# SAQQARA

# SAQQARA

## The Royal Cemetery of Memphis

Excavations and Discoveries since 1850

JEAN-PHILIPPE LAUER

with 210 illustrations, 20 in colour

CHARLES SCRIBNER'S SONS
NEW YORK

Library of Congress Catalog Card Number 75–33508
ISBN 0–684–14551–0

# Contents

# Foreword

The spirit of sacrifice and austerity which characterizes the life of the truly great scholar is worthy of the admiration of all.

I shall always remember the occasion in 1958 when M. Jean-Philippe Lauer first came to call on me in my official capacity as Assistant to the President of the United Arab Republic for Cultural Affairs. Returning to Egypt for the first time since the Suez war of 1956, he wanted to resume his interrupted work on the funerary complex of King Zoser at Saqqara, and his deep seriousness and determination impressed me so greatly that I could not but accede to his request. In the years that I have known him, he has spent at least six months every year, from November to April, in Egypt, devoting himself so completely to his work at Saqqara, that he can truly be said to know the history of each individual stone there.

M. Lauer's work has added a new dimension to the famous funerary complex of King Zoser to which so many distinguished Egyptologists have already devoted themselves. He has spent more than forty years of his life excavating the monuments, clearing their surroundings and restoring them, using nothing but the blocks of stone found on the site itself. It is to his efforts, indeed, that we owe the present appearance of the Step Pyramid at Saqqara and the buildings associated with it; his efforts have earned him the profound gratitude of all visitors – archaeologists, historians, artists and tourists alike.

The present volume in which M. Lauer recounts his campaign to set the architecture of Egypt in the time of King Zoser in its proper perspective is the fruit of a lifetime's work. It is important, however, not only as a work of archaeological interest, but as a vivid personal record of his life among the monuments of Saqqara. The reader is made to participate in M. Lauer's own triumph as, stone by stone, he resuscitates the architecture of this ancient site.

At the same time, M. Lauer reviews the principal activities of the scholars and archaeologists who either preceded him at Saqqara, or whom he has known there personally, and with some of whom he has worked on various occasions. He describes Mariette's excavations at the Serapeum, the first discoveries of the 'Pyramid Texts' by Maspero, the wide-ranging and methodical diggings supervised by Quibell, Jéquier and particularly by Firth, to whom we owe the discovery of the monuments of Zoser, and by Emery who brought to light the Ist Dynasty necropolis, and, last but not least, the valuable researches made by Egyptian architects and archaeologists such as Abdel-Salam M. Hussein or M. Zakaria Goneim whose work was unfortunately interrupted by their premature deaths.

M. Lauer is, however, not only famous for his work on the Step Pyramid complex. In collaboration with Professor J. Leclant of the Sorbonne, he has conducted detailed researches and excavations at the pyramid of Teti and then at those of Pepi I and Merenre in which very numerous fragments engraved with magnificent hieroglyphs from the walls of the burial chambers were gathered; these new elements are valuable additions to Maspero's 'Pyramid Texts', the earliest religious texts known, and on the re-editing of which Professor Leclant is at present actively engaged.

The Lauer-Leclant excavations at South Saqqara have thus been an invaluable counterpart to the work of the late Professor Emery who likewise devoted himself to the monuments of the Old Kingdom and, specifically, to the search for the tomb of Imhotep, the celebrated and deified architect of the Pharaoh Zoser.

This varied and brilliantly illustrated work is both a fascinating account of Old Kingdom archaeology in Egypt and of a lifetime's experience. I feel privileged to be able to introduce the reader to M. Lauer's work.

Saroite Okacha

*Overleaf*
Fig. 1. General site plan of Saqqara (northern sector), showing principal monuments and mastabas discussed in the text.

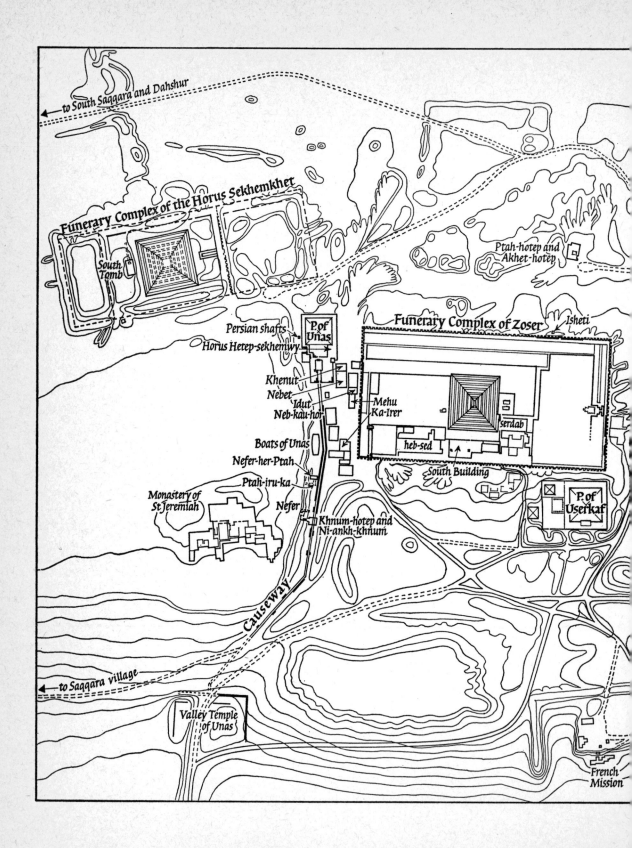

to South Saqqara and Dahshur

Funerary Complex of the Horus Sekhemkhet

South Tomb

Ptah-hotep and Akhet-hotep

Funerary Complex of Zoser

Isheti

Persian shafts

Horus Hetep-sekhemwy

P. of Unas

Khenut

Nebet

Idut

Neb-kau-hor

Mehu

Ka-Irer

serdab

heb-sed

Boats of Unas

Nefer-her-Ptah

Ptah-iru-ka

Monastery of St Jeremiah

Nefer

Khnum-hotep and Ni-ankh-khnum

South Building

P. of Userkaf

Causeway

to Saqqara village

Valley Temple of Unas

French Mission

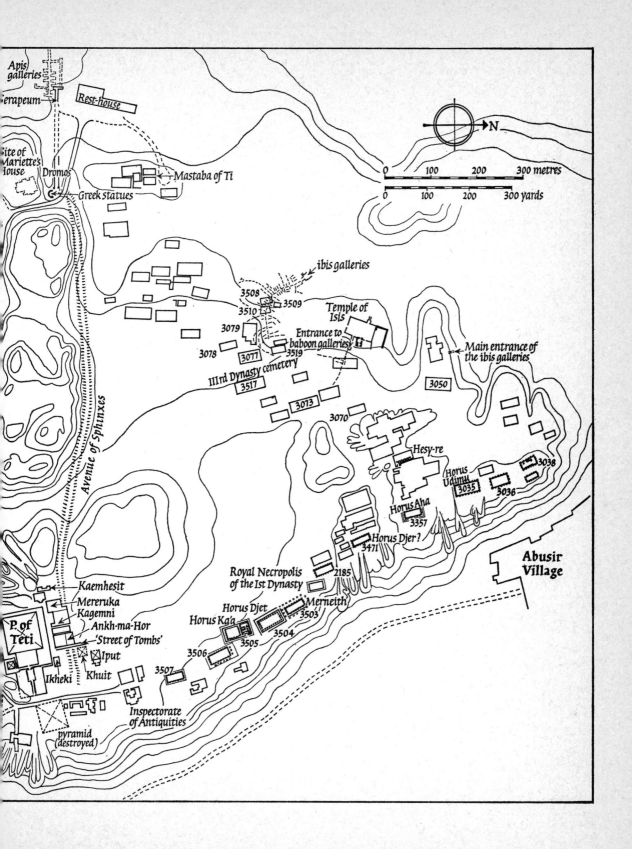

Apis
galleries
Serapeum
Site of
Mariette's
house
Dromos
Greek statues
Rest-house
Mastaba of Ti

N

0    100    200    300 metres
0    100    200    300 yards

ibis galleries
3508
3509
3510
Temple of
Isis
3079
Entrance to
3078          baboon galleries
3077    3519
IIIrd Dynasty cemetery
3517
3013
3070
3050
Main entrance of
the ibis galleries

3038
Hesy-re
Horus
Udimu
3035       3036
Horus Aha
3357
Horus Djer?
3471
Royal Necropolis
of the Ist Dynasty    2185

Abusir
Village

Avenue of Sphinxes

Kaemhesit
Mereruka
Kagemni
Ankh-ma-Hor
P. of
Teti
'Street of Tombs'
Iput
Ikheki    Khuit
Horus Djet    Merneith
Horus Ka'a    3503
3504
3506    3505
3507
Inspectorate
of Antiquities
pyramid
(destroyed)

# Chronological Table:

| Dates (approx.) | Period | Dynasty |
|---|---|---|
| 3100–2900 BC | Thinite | Ist |
| 2900–2730 BC | | IInd |
| 2730–2650 BC | Old Kingdom | IIIrd |
| 2650–2500 BC | | IVth |
| 2500–2350 BC | | Vth |
| 2350–2190 BC | | VIth |
| 2190–2160 BC | | VIIth VIIIth |

# Introduction

In the desert, at the edge of the Libyan plateau facing the cultivated land and the picturesque palm groves that cover the few scattered remains of what was Memphis, the capital city of Old Kingdom Egypt, lies Saqqara, the centre of an immense necropolis.

Except for a few interruptions, this necropolis covers a distance of some fifty kilometres along the edge of the Nile Valley, from the cliffs of Abu Roash that, to the north of the Pyramids of Giza, dominate the apex of the Nile Delta, to Lisht in the south on the way to Upper Egypt.

The name Saqqara, also given to the principal village situated nearby, appears to derive from Sokkar, Memphis' god of the dead. The necropolis of Memphis itself covers an area some eight kilometres long and between 500 and 1,500 metres wide, and it extends from the Abusir pyramids, in the north, to those of Dahshur in the south, these being, in fact, but extensions to it.

Though the archaeological importance of the site is now, like that of Thebes (modern Luxor) in upper Egypt, one of the highlights of the civilization and the arts of ancient Egypt, it remained practically unsuspected during the first half of the nineteenth century. In fact, only the majestic Step Pyramid of Zoser (or Djeser) which dominates the whole area, had been the object of investigations of a more or less archaeological nature. The first of these had been undertaken in 1821 by the Prussian General von Minutoli with the help of Segato, an Italian engineer. Sixteen years later, the engineer J. S. Perring carried out some excavations on behalf of Colonel Howard Vyse and did some remarkable drawings of the pyramid and its deep galleries. Finally, in 1842–3, the German Egyptologist Richard Lepsius, having in his turn explored the monument, removed a door lintel and frame carved with the king's name and the adjacent panel decorated with small blue tiles, and took them to the Berlin Museum.

It was not until 1851, following Auguste Mariette's sensational discovery of the Serapeum (discussed in Chapter I), a subterranean gallery in which the sacred Apis bulls were buried, that the attention of scholars and other interested people was really drawn to this ancient site which was to prove so rich and so rewarding. I hope to demonstrate its riches by evoking and describing the principal discoveries – often astounding – that have been made at Saqqara in the course of over a century of excavation and research.

Before describing in detail the different stages of the excavations and the contribution to our knowledge made by each of them, and in order to help the reader appreciate their value and interest, it may be useful to throw some light on certain very individual aspects of Egyptian civilization, and especially on the beliefs held by the ancient Egyptians about death and about life in the hereafter, since these beliefs gave rise to so many beautiful works and so many wonderful achievements.

Essentially, most of our knowledge about ancient Egypt comes from the tombs: they were built on the desert plateau – on sites out of reach of the annual inundation of the Nile – for eternity. Their construction had, therefore, to be as solid and durable as possible and, at a very early date, stone came to be used first by the kings and, soon afterwards, by important officials who could afford it. The first great monumental funerary complex built of dressed stone was the work of Imhotep, the celebrated vizier-architect of King Zoser, in the IIIrd Dynasty, *c.* 2700 BC.

The discovery of this complex by Cecil M. Firth, between 1924 and 1927, and the restoration subsequently carried out upset the generally accepted theory of the origin of stone architecture in Egypt – that it had derived from megalithic monuments. The architecture of the IIIrd Dynasty developed directly from crude brick construction, retaining the arrangement of courses with frequent alternation of headers and stretchers, together with the use of relatively small blocks. This masonry also imitated in stone, but in a purely symbolic manner, the shapes and elements of earlier light structures made of rush matting, reeds or of wood. The whole Step Pyramid complex contained numerous representations in stone of wooden doors, either open or closed.

King Zoser's palace and the palaces of his successors, however, were built in the valley and must certainly have been made of mud bricks. Thus each new pharaoh could build, much more rapidly than would be possible in stone, and on a site of his choice, a suitable residence which would last only for his own lifetime.

In considering the concept of human life, it is important to remember that, for the ancient Egyptians, a man consisted not only of his body and soul (the latter represented in the form of the human-headed *ba* bird) but also of the *ka* which was supposed to have the exact appearance of the individual, for whom it was thus a sort of double, and was at the same time the vital force given to him at birth. If this *ka* happened to leave him, it meant immediate death. This fact accounts for all the efforts made to retain the *ka* near the body of the deceased, particularly by the more or less magical rites of mummification. Its permanent preservation thus ensured, the body, provided that it was kept in a safe place, would continue to serve as a support for the *ka* and thus recover its vital force. Hence the myth of the divine king Osiris who, after being murdered by his evil brother Seth, was restored to life and ruled over the Underworld, while his son Horus – the divine falcon and protector of the king, with whom each successive pharaoh was identified – ruled over the living. This miraculous restoration was due to the efforts of Isis, his widow, who (with the help of the jackal-headed god Anubis) found and re-assembled the pieces of Osiris' dismembered body.

In the tomb, regarded as the 'house of eternity', the mummified deceased, having 'returned to his *ka*', came back to life on condition that he received the necessary food, which had to be brought to him by his family or by the priests in charge of the funerary cult. However, because they defaulted too often, 'imitative magic' was resorted to at an early date and suitable carved scenes or statues were provided. Thus, a false door stela, its frame carved with the formula of offerings followed by the name, titles and portrait of the deceased, would be placed in front of the deep shaft leading to the burial chamber. The *ka* was supposed to be able to 'come out at the voice' through the false door and partake of the provisions placed on an offerings table before it. If these provisions were not there, the *ka* had the magical power to make use of whatever was mentioned on the stela above the false door (on which the deceased was depicted seated in front of a table with his hand on a cake cut in several pieces) and, later, of everything listed or depicted on the walls of the offerings chamber or on those of the burial chamber.

This was the main purpose of the magnificent scenes in low relief which, from the beginning of the IVth Dynasty, decorated the mastabas (tombs resembling in outline the mud benches seen in front of village houses in Egypt) of nobles, and soon after, of those of officials or other lesser persons. These scenes, at first nearly always limited to the bringing of offerings, later became much more varied, especially under the Vth and VIth Dynasties. They would depict most of the daily activities of the owner of the tomb so that his *ka* could re-live them for ever thanks to the magical powers of the pictures placed at his disposal. The reliefs generally represented the deceased with his wife at his side and his children at his feet, and only during the happier moments of his life carefully chosen for the *ka*. I cannot do better than quote from Alexandre Moret's *Au temps des pharaons* (pp. 183–4), in which he has authoritatively explained the meaning of the development of these scenes: 'All around, servants bring provisions of food, clothing and the necessary furniture; the making and origin of each offering is used as the theme for the decoration. Thus, to explain the offering of a leg of beef, they show animals feeding in the pasture, the mounting of the cow, the birth of the calf and scenes of agricultural life up to the slaughter of the animal; the offering of bread made it necessary to have scenes of tilling, harvesting and baking; the offering of wine was the excuse to show vineyards and grape-gathering; offerings of furred and feathered game and of fish made it necessary to show scenes of hunting in the desert and of fishing by line or net. Each of the objects of the funerary furniture – shrine, coffin, bed, vessels, clothing, arms or jewels – gave rise to descriptions of the methods of manufacture of these objects; thus, we can see, plying their trades, carpenters, foundrymen, armourers, weavers and jewellers. Even the purchase of provisions in the market and the drawing up of household accounts are used as decorative subjects. The soul and the body of the deceased re-lived perpetually the sculpted scenes: the act depicted became a reality, each picture of a being or an object recaptured, for a moment, its *ka* and came to life according to the wish of the god who lived in the tomb . . .'

Other scenes also adorned these mastabas. Some of them, especially those showing pastimes, must have been of great importance because they ensured that the deceased was provided with the necessary amusements. Thus, he may be represented playing board games, listening to music played on the harp or flute, watching dancers or young people at sporting games or even boatmen jousting, etc. Lastly, for very important people, the progress of the owner in his canopied litter is often shown, and sometimes we see the bearers exclaim: 'We would rather carry the litter full than empty!'

In view of the extreme care taken over even the smallest details in these many different scenes, we can only conclude that every owner of one of these beautifully appointed tombs must have felt extreme satisfaction, while closely supervising the building and decoration of his intended resting place, in seeing himself thus represented on each wall, engaged in his various lordly or family activities.

Indeed, it is also very probable that, after the death of the owner, his relatives and friends must have derived great comfort from gathering together on certain occasions in front of such scenes, perhaps to have a meal or banquet in memory of the deceased, a practice still prevalent today, in modern Islamic Egypt.

The royal pyramids of the second half of the Old Kingdom were also mostly built at Saqqara. Although their funerary temples – exploited as quarries from the earliest times – have unfortunately been largely destroyed, the excavations undertaken have often brought to light important remains that have made it possible to reconstruct their ground plans; also, many sculptures and reliefs have been found showing not only agricultural scenes and craftsmen at work, as already revealed by the mastabas, but also numerous other scenes more proper to the king's funerary cult. He is now considered as the son of Re, the sun god, and, like Re, a god on equal terms with the other gods. In his three-volume work on Pepi II's funerary temple, Gustave Jéquier writes of these gods: 'Their role is reduced to welcoming the pharaoh in his funerary domain, to adopt him as one of them, to protect him and to accompany him during his outings . . .' In none of the temple pictures is the king shown praying or doing homage or making an offering to any divinity; on the contrary, they all stress his own divine prerogatives.

Among the scenes concerning the royal funerary cult, the most notable concerns the *heb-sed* (the pharaoh's jubilee festival, originating at the beginning of the Ist Dynasty), during which the renewal of the royal powers and prerogatives was celebrated with great solemnity.

Other elements concern various rites, such as the very ancient one of the erection of the mast; the embracing of the king by the goddess Hathor; the king's reception by the goddesses Nekhbet and Edjo, patrons respectively of Upper and Lower Egypt; the king being suckled by a goddess; processions of divinities or dignitaries and courtiers; and triumphal scenes showing prisoners being massacred by the pharaoh himself as an affirmation of his authority, etc.

Lastly we note, among the scenes decorating the walls of the causeway leading to the mortuary temple beside the pyramid, those depicting the return of expeditions of sea-going ships whose crews and the foreign prisoners or slaves they are bringing back acclaim the king; and others depicting the transportation on barges from Elephantine Island, the traditional southern boundary of Egypt, of columns and other large granite monoliths for the funerary temple.

The earliest inscriptions in the burial chambers of the pyramids occur in the pyramid of Unas, the last king of the Vth Dynasty; these are the famous 'Pyramid Texts' discovered by Gaston Maspero in 1881. The texts – additional and variant examples of which we are at present seeking in the VIth Dynasty pyramids exploited as quarries in the Middle Ages – opened up new horizons. Here was fresh information about the mythology and beliefs of the ancient Egyptians concerning the life of the king in the hereafter; and new light was shed on writing, language and grammar, because the priests of Heliopolis (centre of the sun-cult) had assembled the texts from diverse sources, often going back to periods considerably earlier than the Old Kingdom. We find that these priests succeeded in amalgamating the cult of Osiris, as applicable to common mortals, with the solar doctrine of their god Atum-Re, who was cosmic in character. Thanks to these texts – which must have had, in the eyes of the priests, strong magical powers – the deceased king would, by uttering these inscribed formulas, be able more surely to surmount all the obstacles that might prevent him from rising to heaven, to reach the solar barque of Re and reign with him over gods and men.

If we leave the pyramids and mastabas of the Old Kingdom and go to the northern sector of Saqqara towards the Serapeum, burial place of the Apis bulls, we make a leap forward in time of some sixteen centuries. The vast underground galleries there were started about the middle of the seventh century BC by Psammetichus I, founder of the XXVIth Dynasty. The discovery of the Serapeum by Auguste Mariette in 1851 – the precursor of all the many subsequent discoveries – was an event of the first magnitude for Egyptologists, leaving aside the simple fact of the discovery of the huge tombs of these strange Apis (or Hapi) bulls which had previously been known only from references to them by various writers of antiquity.

This, in particular, is what the Greek traveller Herodotus wrote (*Histories*, III, 28): 'This Apis is a young calf, born of a cow which is unable thereafter to conceive other offspring. And the Egyptians say that fire descends upon the cow from heaven, and by this she conceives Apis. This calf is called Apis, and its marks are these: it is black, with a white square upon the brow, the likeness of an eagle on the back, double hairs on the tail, and the likeness of a scarab underneath the tongue . . .' Apis thus miraculously conceived was considered to be an incarnation of Ptah, the god of Memphis. Worshipped as such during his life-time within a special sanctuary in the temple of Ptah, he was mummified after his death in this very temple in which there still exist at Memphis two huge alabaster monoliths used as tables for the purpose of mummification. After mummification, being then identified with Osiris under the name of Osiris-Apis (or Osorapis), he was taken with great pomp to his last resting place prepared for him in the Serapeum.

For the Greeks these ceremonies for the funeral of Osiris-Apis must have presented great similarities with certain ceremonies connected with Dionysos, the god of wine and of the Mysteries, since Herodotus wrote (*Histories*, II, 144): 'Osiris is he who is called Dionysos in the Greek tongue.' This assimilation must have later have greatly facilitated that of Osorapis with the Hellenistic god Serapis, after whom the Serapeum was named and who was also closely associated with Dionysos. This syn-cretization was desired by Ptolemy I with the object of founding in Memphis a cult area that would enable Egyptians and Greeks alike to join in a community of beliefs acceptable to each, and at the same time give those Greeks who had established them-selves in Egypt rites sufficiently Hellenistic for them to consider acceptable.

This co-existence of the two cults seems to have worked very well, thanks to Serapis-Dionysos who, for the Egyptians, was none other than Osorapis. Diodorus (II, 96) admits, in fact, that there is 'only the difference in names between the festivals of Bacchus and those of Osiris, between the Mysteries of Isis and those of Demeter', and Plutarch (*Isis and Osiris*, 35) adds: 'That Osiris is the same as Dionysos, and who should know better than you, Clea, since you are at once the leader of the Thyades [female initiates who celebrated on sacred sites the nocturnal orgies of Bacchus] at Delphi and have been consecrated in the Isirian rites by your father and mother?'

Thus is explained the astonishing intrusion of Greek statuary and architecture in the 'dromos' (the name given by Mariette, following Strabo, to the paved avenue) which, coming after the long avenue of sphinxes in purely Egyptian style, leads to the entrance of the Serapeum's underground galleries. Plutarch also says (*ibid.*, 35) on this subject: '. . . as for what the priests openly do in the burial of the Apis when they transport its carcass on a raft,[1] this in no way falls short of Bacchic revelry, for they wear fawn-skins[2] and carry thyrsus-rods[3] and produce shouts and movements as do the ecstatic celebrants of the Dionysiac orgies . . .'

The retinue of sacred animals ridden by Dionysos as a child or as a young man, discussed in Chapter I (see Plates 8, 9), shows that proper Dionysiac rites were practised there and proves without doubt the establishment in Egypt of the cult of Serapis and of Greek ideas by Ptolemy I at the beginning of the third century B.C. This is also the case with the strange semicircle of Greek poets and philosophers erected at the junction of the avenue of sphinxes with the *dromos* (Plates 2, 5). This semicircle cannot be a Hellenistic tomb evoking portraits of famous people, nor, as has been suggested, simply an offering to beautify the processional route; it is undoubtedly a monument sacred to Dionysos. Various surviving buildings of classical antiquity show that philosophical schools and groups of poets were frequently created near necropolises and sacred burial grounds. Plato's Academy in Athens was situated, from the first half of the fourth century B.C, near Colonus, according to Sophocles the burial place of Oedipus. And was not meditation about death the main theme of the researches of sages? Gathered here at Saqqara, as in a Dionysian *stibadeion*,[4] the group of poets and philosophers, presided over by Homer, was not at all unexpected or out of place at the start of the *dromos* of Serapis (Osorapis) where the procession of sacred animals ridden by Dionysos was found.

However, the Serapeum complex, called the 'House of Osorapis' by the Egyptians, also contained many elements other than the avenue of sphinxes, the dromos, and the underground galleries where the Apis bulls were buried. Mariette's excavations led to the discovery first of the small temple, built in the fourth century B.C by Nectanebo II and dedicated to Osorapis, immediately to the east of the Greek semi-circle; then, nearer the valley, of numerous constructions in mud bricks, which have since partly disappeared, and which he called the Greek Serapeum – mistakenly, however, because the remains, situated within the very thick and vast enclosing wall that is still visible, formed the domain of purely Egyptian gods: Anubis, Bastet and, perhaps, Imhotep, identified by the Greeks with Asclepios, the god of medicine.

The Anubieion (temple of Anubis) comprised, in addition to the temple itself, a gallery of tomb-niches for dogs, quarters for the representative of the governor of Memphis, a police station, a prison, offices, inns for the numerous pilgrims, and four structures called 'Chambers of Bes' in which strange statues of this god were found by J. E. Quibell.

No trace of the presumed remains of the Bubasteion (temple of Bastet) has been found within the enclosing wall protecting the galleries in which numerous mummies of cats, sacred to the cat-headed goddess Bastet, were found.

Whether the site of the Asclepieon, the temple of Imhotep, is in this sector at the very edge of the valley is a matter of pure supposition; it could just as easily be situated either nearer the complex of the Step Pyramid built by Imhotep or – in view of the affinity that seems to have existed between this healing god and scholar and Thoth, the great god of science and writing – near the temple of Thoth, the site of which (800 metres to the north of the Serapeum) has recently been discovered during the search for Imhotep's tomb undertaken for the Egypt Exploration Society by our late colleague and friend Walter B. Emery.

Near this temple of Thoth, Emery discovered a vast network of galleries containing several thousand ibises carefully mummified and stacked (which had already been glimpsed in the eighteenth century by the French traveller Paul Lucas), and then other galleries containing baboons, falcons or other birds of prey, also carefully mummified. Lastly, a little further north, he discovered the remains of the Isieion, the temple of Isis, mother of Apis, with underground galleries containing the sarcophagi of the sacred cows that had borne and given birth to the Apis bulls.

All these various animal cults grouped within the immense complex of the Serapeum must have attracted a considerable number of pilgrims who came to invoke either Osorapis or other divinities such as Thoth, Imhotep, Isis, Horus, Anubis, Bastet, etc., and for the Greeks (from the time of Ptolemy I), Serapis-Dionysos; this accounts for the presence of the various secular buildings near the Anubieion mentioned above.

We do not know with any degree of certainty the reason for these labyrinths of galleries containing the thousands of mummified birds and sacred animals. Nevertheless it seems possible to presume that the postulant seeking a cure or the fulfilment of a wish was required, among other things, to make an offering of a mummified bird or animal sacred to the god invoked, a pious gesture that was likely to draw favours; or that one whose prayer had been granted made such an offering as an ex-voto to the beneficent god.

Only the study now taking place of the numerous written documents, collected during these latest excavations by the Egypt Exploration Society, will provide definitive answers to the questions raised by these strange animal cults that developed so much during the Late Egyptian period.

# The Serapeum and Mariette's First Discoveries

At the end of April 1850, Auguste Mariette, at that time attached to the Louvre's Department of Egyptian Antiquities, obtained, after lengthy efforts, an official Mission to Egypt: he was granted a credit of 6,000 francs to negotiate, on behalf of France, the purchase of ancient manuscripts from Coptic monasteries.

After many detours at sea, Mariette arrived in Alexandria on 2 October. He immediately began to make, both there and in Cairo, contacts with the Coptic ecclesiastical authorities. In spite, however, of the help of the French consul-general Le Moyne and of French personalities such as Linant Bey (Linant de Bellefonds) and Dr Clot Bey,[5] he was unable to obtain the necessary permits. The Coptic Patriarchate was extremely reluctant to issue them because of certain dishonest acquisitions made earlier by some unscrupulous scholars. While the negotiations were going on, Mariette, availing himself of the opportunity afforded him by the delays, visited the antiquity shops. He noticed that several of them possessed similar sphinxes and was told that they all came from the Saqqara necropolis.

The idea of going in search of pharaonic antiquities – something he had entertained for a long time – again entered his mind and the disappointing visit he paid to the Patriarchate on 17 October only served to strengthen the idea. After a night of deliberation, he climbed up to the Citadel where he stayed until evening absorbed in thought: 'the stillness,' he wrote, 'was extraordinary. At my feet lay the city. Upon it a thick and heavy fog seemed to have settled covering all the houses to the roof-tops. From this deep sea rose three hundred minarets like masts from some submerged fleet. Far away, towards the south, one could perceive the palm groves that rise from the fallen ruins of Memphis. To the west, bathed in the gold and flaming dust of the sunset, were the pyramids. The view was superb. It held me and absorbed me with a violence that was almost painful. The moment was decisive. Before my eyes lay Giza, Abusir, Saqqara, Dahshur, Mit-Rahineh. This life-long dream of mine was materializing. Over there, practically within my grasp, was a whole world of tombs, stelae, inscriptions, statues. What more can I say? The next day I hired two or three mules for my luggage, one or two donkeys for myself; I had bought a tent, a few cases of provisions, all the necessities for a trip to the desert and, on 20 October 1850, I pitched my tent at the foot of the Great Pyramid . . .'[6]

After visiting the site of the pyramids of Giza where some Bedouins were digging, he proceeded, on 27 October, to the necropolis of Saqqara which he began to explore. One day, while walking around, tape-measure in hand, trying to unravel the plan of the tombs, he noticed, barely emerging from the sand, a limestone head with features that were strangely reminiscent of those of the sphinxes he had admired in Cairo. He tells us that, immediately, a quotation from Strabo[7] came to his mind: ' "One finds [at Memphis]," said the geographer, "a temple to Serapis in such a sandy place that the wind heaps up sand dunes beneath which we saw sphinxes, some half-buried, some buried up to the head, from which one can suppose that the way to this temple could not be without danger if one were caught in a sudden wind-storm."[8] Did it not seem that Strabo had written this sentence to help us rediscover, after over eighteen centuries, the famous temple dedicated to Serapis? It was impossible to doubt it. This buried sphinx, the companion of fifteen others I had encountered in Alexandria and Cairo, formed, with them, according to the evidence, part of the avenue that led to the Memphis Serapeum.'

As the Patriarchate's letter had not arrived, Mariette thought he would use the few days he had available to follow the avenue of sphinxes and reach the monument. 'It did not seem to me possible,' he wrote, 'to leave to others the credit and the profit of exploring this temple whose remains a fortunate chance had allowed me to discover and whose location would henceforth be known. Undoubtedly many precious fragments, many statues, many unknown texts were hidden beneath the sands upon which I stood. These considerations made all my scruples disappear. At that instant I forgot my mission, I forgot the Patriarch, the convents, the Coptic and Syriac manuscripts, Linant Bey himself, and it was thus, on 1 November 1850, during one of the most beautiful sunrises I had ever seen in Egypt, that a group of some thirty workmen, working under my orders near that sphinx, were about to cause such a total upheaval in the conditions of my stay in Egypt.'[9]

*Pl. 1*

Having then uncovered several of these sphinxes lying at six-metre intervals, Mariette thought that the direction taken by the avenue at that point could allow him to determine approximately the site of the Serapeum. But the work took time. The slightly sinuous alley (see Fig. 1) was often buried under ten metres of sand and debris which forced him to widen the excavation considerably. It was during one of these widenings that the tomb of Sekhem-ka was discovered which yielded, in addition to seven limestone statues of the owner, the Louvre's well-known 'Squatting Scribe', one of the masterpieces of Egyptian statuary.     *Pl. 29*

One hundred and thirty-four sphinxes were thus successively uncovered and then the avenue seemed to end. Actually it swerved abruptly to the south in a semi-circle and this fact was eventually revealed by the positioning of a sphinx placed at right-angles to the others. Then, a few metres further away, Mariette was astonished to find, instead of another sphinx, a beautiful Hellenistic limestone statue of a man playing a lyre     *Pls. 3, 4* and seated on a sumptuous chair from which hung, on each side, two lion-skins sculpted in the stone. At that time the name Pindarus (the Greek poet Pindar, 518–438 BC) could still be read on the base, but the inscription is indecipherable today.

Immediately beyond this statue, ten other statues were uncovered. More mutilated than the first and in pure Hellenistic style, they were arranged in a semi-circle; Plato, Protagoras and     *Pl. 2* Homer are represented, the latter being placed in the centre of the group over which he seems to preside.[10]

Although thoroughly disconcerted by this discovery (which explains his severe and unjust criticism of the quality of these works that were, nevertheless, so precious in so many ways), Mariette did not allow himself to be deterred and courageously resumed his excavations. Next he found, towards the east, at the entrance to a thirty-metre-wide courtyard, two sphinxes, larger than those in the avenue, bearing the name of Nectanebo II of the XXXth Dynasty, the last native pharaoh. In the centre of the courtyard lay an overturned statue (now in the Louvre) of the beneficent god Bes. He immediately set it upright and     *Pl. 6* described it as follows: 'The god is standing, his fat hands on his hips, his beard curled, his mouth wide open. For a belt he wears a snake. He is squat and grotesque . . . It is the hour for the midday meal and the sun beats straight down upon the statue making the details stand out in powerful relief. Women from Abusir and Saqqara have arrived to join our workmen. A sort of procession is formed. It is evident that they take Bes for the devil. The procession starts and each one acts according to their character. The women stand in front of the statue and revile it with mad gestures; the workmen mostly spit on it. Among them I have two or three Negroes, who stare at the impassive god then run off with shouts of laughter . . .'[11]

Beyond the courtyard lay the ruins of a small temple with a few reliefs that showed it to have been dedicated to the god Apis (Osorapis) by Nectanebo II. Mariette was now convinced that he was on the right track. He made some soundings towards the west of the semi-circle and reached, some eighty metres beyond, the base of a pylon preceded by a paved way which obviously joined it to the temple, and which he designated 'the dromos'. Two fine limestone lions, carved with the name of Nectanebo I, of the XXXth Dynasty, guarded the entrance pylon, and some of its fallen cornice blocks showed that it had been erected by that king. On each side of the pylon were some elements of an open-work stone barrier that must have formed an enclosure.

*Pl. 7*

After a few days' interruption to collect more funds, Mariette undertook the clearing of the *dromos* which was bordered by two low walls of dressed stone. These he named, using the Arabic word, the mastabas of the north and of the south. Discovery then followed upon discovery, each as astonishing as the last.[12] First found, on the southern mastaba, were the Tura limestone statues of a panther and two strutting peacocks, each ridden by Dionysos as a child or an adolescent; to these were added a falcon with the head of a bearded man, a sphinx and the remains of a long-haired mermaid, and, on the pavement itself, appeared a majestic lion astride a fountain, trampling vines and bunches of grapes, and ridden by a young Dionysos (only the legs, wearing Thracian sandals, remained). On the northern mastaba, towards its northern extremity, was a powerful Cerberus with a leonine middle head and a tail ending in a snake-head, also ridden by a young Dionysos. Finally, towards its western side were two adjoining chapels, one Egyptian in style and the other Corinthian. The first housed a magnificent limestone statue of an Apis bull painted with its characteristic markings.[13] It caused, like the statue of Bes, picturesque demonstrations, this time mostly by the women of the neighbourhood. Shortly after this discovery and during the workmen's lunch hour, Mariette came upon some fifteen women of all ages in turn mounting the bull. He was told that this exercise was a way to overcome their sterility!

*Pls. 3, 5*

*Pl. 8*

*Pl. 9*

*Pl. 10*

Towards the end of April, Mariette was obliged to interrupt

his work for a few weeks, having contracted a severe eye in-
fection. He therefore had a house built to shelter him from the
elements and to store his finds safely. It was this crude brick
house which, under the name of 'Mariette's house', was still
being used a century later as a shelter for tourists. It was, alas,
pulled down in 1958 and replaced by a large building, much too
important and ostentatious, that was supposed to serve both as
a rest-house and a museum but which, due to faulty foundations, was soon to become useless.

When Mariette was able to resume work, he thought that
perhaps the entrance to the Serapeum was hidden beneath the
paving of the *dromos*. Instead he was surprised to find bronze
statues of Egyptian divinities; he therefore had the paving removed entirely but was later, unfortunately, unable to reinstate
it. However, several hundred statuettes and amulets were
brought to light. The grossly exaggerated news of this discovery
– it was rumoured that there were several thousand figurines
not of bronze but of solid gold – caused a great deal of excite-
ment and Mariette was ordered by the Egyptian Government
to stop his excavations.

After some negotiations, work was resumed on 30 June and
if was only on 12 November 1851 that Mariette was able to
penetrate the great burial galleries of the Apis bulls, and this at
a time when fresh administrative difficulties were to paralyse
the diggings until mid-February 1852.

At the very entrance of the Serapeum, many small votive
stelae littered the ground; even more of them covered the rock-
walls of the great excavation that led, southwards, into the
principal gallery over two hundred metres long. On each side of          *Pl. 11*
this gallery opened out vast chambers excavated at right-angles
to it and below its floor level; each contained one of twenty-four
huge granite sarcophagi that had been placed there between the          *Pl. 12*
fifty-second year of the reign of Psammetichus I, founder of the
XXVIth Dynasty in 663 BC, and the end of the Ptolemaic
period in 30 BC. The lids of these sarcophagi had been systematically pushed back or broken, undoubtedly by the Coptic
monks of the monastery of St Jeremiah situated in Saqqara
itself, with the object of suppressing pagan pilgrimages by
removing the remains of the bulls.

When the excavations were resumed, other galleries were
found. They were just as large but more disordered and dated
back to more ancient times. They contained wooden sarcophagi
of sacred bulls of the XIXth to XXIInd Dynasties, the earliest

dating from the thirtieth year of the reign of Ramesses II. Near the centre of the gallery an enormous rock blocked the way. It had to be cleared by the use of explosives. Underneath it, deeply embedded in the ground, was a wooden sarcophagus of which only the lid had been crushed; the mummy it contained was intact. It was not that of a bull but of a man. 'A golden mask covered his face,' wrote Mariette, 'a small column of green felspar and a red jasper ring hung by a gold chain round his neck. Another gold chain carried two amulets of jasper, all in the name of Prince Kha-em-wase, son of Ramesses II. An admirable hawk with open wings in gold and cloisonné mosaics lay on his breast. Eighteen human-headed statuettes inscribed "Osiris-Apis, great god, lord of eternity" were scattered around . . .' It was evidently the coffin of Prince Kha-em-wase himself who, being governor of Memphis and high-priest of Ptah, had wanted to be buried among the Apis bulls; this was confirmed by Mariette's discovery of a large granite stela in his name lying near the entrance to the Serapeum.

*Pl. 13*

Between 15 March and 5 September 1852, Mariette found, within the area of the Serapeum, a third series of Apis tombs, scattered here and there and not placed in a regular pattern, and dating from the XVIIIth to the first half of the XIXth Dynasty. All had been plundered with the exception of one that was intact and very rich; Mariette was greatly moved, on entering, to find in the layer of dust that covered the floor, footprints of the priests who had laid the divine bull to rest in its coffin 3,000 years before.[14] He then found himself facing two great wooden sarcophagi, rectangular, and painted black. The gold-leaf that had covered their lids and sides had fallen off. A handsome stela told of the death of these two Apis, one in the sixteenth and the other in the twenty-sixth year of the king. Near one of these sarcophagi were four large alabaster canopic jars with human-headed lids, and near the other a life-size standing statue of the god Osiris made of gilded wood. Niches in the chamber walls held two sandstone statues of Prince Kha-em-wase, painted red and blue, and two pylon-like altars each topped by a figure of Anubis, the god-jackal, and containing four glazed earthenware figurines. On the surfaces one could distinguish two pictures in both of which Ramesses II and his son Kha-em-wase are shown making libations before two Apis, represented in human form as Osiris. On raising the lids of these sarcophagi, Mariette was greatly surprised to find that they contained only a smelly bituminous mass that fell to dust at the slightest touch. It covered a quantity of small bones, broken at the time of the bull's burial, but there was no trace of the animal's head.

In one of these sarcophagi, mingled with the bones, were fifteen bull-headed funerary statuettes inscribed with the name of the dead Apis, some ten gold objects engraved with the names of Kha-em-wase and other dignitaries of Memphis, and statuettes in greenish schist representing the prince himself or other princes of the royal family, and, lastly, finely carved amulets in cornelian, red quartz and serpentine, and a large quantity of gold-leaf.

In the other sarcophagus, among the broken bones, Mariette picked up a beautiful pectoral, *naos*-shaped, in gold with inlays in coloured glass, bearing the prenomen in a cartouche of Ramesses II, and six bull-headed funerary statuettes, but no other amulets.

*Pl. 14*

Mariette's funds were now running out; fortunately the exhibition of the Serapeum jewels held in the Louvre enabled the management of the National Museums of France to obtain an important new grant for him and, consequently, the excavations were able to continue until 15 September 1853. It was in this way that, among other things, Mariette was able to resume, this time eastward, the exploration of the avenue of sphinxes. It led him to the Pastophorium (domain of the officiating priests) and to the area adjacent to cultivated land.

A considerable number of ancient objects representing all the different periods, from the dawn of the Old Kingdom up to the Roman conquest, and constituting a very great addition to the knowledge of Egyptian civilization and art, had now been collected and Mariette was required to draw up a detailed inventory with a view to sharing his finds with the Egyptian Government. When this was over, two hundred and thirty cases of antiquities – those officially allotted to the Louvre – were shipped to France in two naval frigates specially sent over for that purpose.

In the house on the sands which he had built, Mariette, who was quite unconcerned about personal comfort, had only some very rudimentary furniture made of planks roughly assembled and badly planed. Nevertheless, he was able to live there with his wife and two children for over two years and also to welcome passing visitors. One of these was the German Egyptologist Henri Brugsch whose stay, originally planned for a few days, was to last eight months.

These two men, each as lively and enthusiastic as the other, complemented each other remarkably well from a scientific point of view. Maspero wrote: 'Every morning found each of them at his work as if he had slept all night, one directing the diggings and giving orders to his workmen, the other deciphering monuments and gathering material for his *Demotic Grammar*.'[15] As to Brugsch, this is how, in his memoirs, he describes living conditions in Mariette's house: 'Snakes slithered along the floor, tarantulas or scorpions swarmed in the wall crevices, large spider-webs waved from the ceiling like flags. As soon as night fell, bats, attracted by the light, entered my cell through the cracks in the door and kept me awake with their spectral flights. Before going to sleep, I tucked the edges of my mosquito-net beneath my mattress and put my trust in God and all the saints, while outside jackals, hyenas and wolves howled around the house . . .'[16]

Mariette was indifferent to such discomforts. Indeed, he was sometimes saddened by the thought that he would eventually have to leave this hovel to return to France. He was able to put off this dreaded departure for a year, thanks to an assignment he received from the Duc de Luynes: to verify whether there could be any truth in Pliny's statement that, according to the Egyptians, the Sphinx at Giza could be the tomb of King Harmais.[17] After investigations and observations at the site of the Sphinx had proved negative, he succeeded in uncovering, close by, the great temple lined with slabs of polished red granite (the Valley Temple, part of the IVth Dynasty King Khephren's funerary complex) whose real function he was, at that time, unable to interpret and which he called 'the Temple of the Sphinx'.

He did not succeed, however, in obtaining the necessary additional funds to finish the excavation, which would certainly have led him to the famous diorite statue of Khephren, and so, reluctantly, he embarked with his family for Marseilles on 24 September 1854. 'I arrived thus at the end of the mission I have accomplished in Egypt,' he notes in his report, '. . . I have found no Syriac or Coptic manuscripts, I have not made the inventory of any library, but, stone by stone, I have brought back a temple.'

# The Principal Mastabas and Monuments Discovered by Mariette

Back in France, though very busy studying and preparing for publication his very numerous and many important discoveries, Mariette was unceasingly haunted by his memories of Egypt and gnawed by his longing to resume the excavations: 'I would have died or gone mad if I had not been able to return promptly to Egypt,' he confided to Maspero long afterwards. Happily, he got his chance during the first months of 1857. Prince Napoleon, the French emperor's cousin, had expressed a desire to visit Egypt. Mariette's friends immediately thought of him. Ferdinand de Lesseps, the great French engineer responsible for building the Suez Canal, to whom Mariette had expressed his concern over the neglect of the pharaonic monuments, and to whom he had submitted a plan for their protection, presented this plan to Saïd Pasha, Viceroy of Egypt. He had very skilfully connected the visit to the plan, and the Viceroy accepted that Mariette should go to Egypt and start excavations there in view of the impending royal visit. At the Prince's request, the French Government gave Mariette a scientific commission for eight months and so, by the end of October, Mariette was able to leave for Cairo where he was received with great affability by Saïd Pasha. The Viceroy granted him funds, put at his disposal one of the Court's steamers, the *Samanoud*, and did not hesitate to give him a strongly worded order in the following terms: 'You will ensure the safety of the monuments, you will tell the *mudirs* [governors] of all the provinces that I forbid them to touch one single antique stone; you will imprison any *fellah* [peasant] who sets foot inside a temple.'[18] Mariette immediately established his headquarters at Giza and Saqqara where, he felt sure, there were abundant antiquities. At Saqqara he discovered the fine VIth Dynasty stela of Isi that the Viceroy subsequently presented to Prince Napoleon who, in turn, presented it to the Louvre. It was at this time also that he discovered and opened the 'Mastabat Fara'un', that curious royal tomb built in the shape of a sarcophagus and situated about three kilometres south of the Step Pyramid. He then went to Upper Egypt, returning with an important collection of objects.

Mariette was not unduly disturbed to learn, at the end of July 1858, that Prince Napoleon's journey to Egypt had been postponed indefinitely due to many difficulties. Very cunningly he suggested to his friends in France that if the Prince, to compensate for his missed journey, would express the desire to buy, for his personal collection, some of the antiquities uncovered during the latest excavations, the gesture would be greatly appreciated by the Viceroy. The suggestion was accepted by the Prince and Mariette imparted this desire to Saïd Pasha 'in such a manner that the Viceroy, with his customary generosity,' wrote Maspero, 'refused to listen to any talk of price or indemnity of any kind. He asked Mariette to choose what was most likely to please the Prince and place it at the Prince's disposal . . .'[19] The Prince was delighted and asked Mariette to convey his thanks directly to Saïd Pasha. Soon afterwards, in 1858, the Viceroy, who held Mariette in great esteem, appointed him, in the face of strong opposition, 'Director of Antiquities'.

Mariette now began plans for large-scale excavations. He decided to concentrate on the sites of Memphis (Saqqara and Giza), Abydos, Thebes and Edfu. He kept for himself the management of the excavations at Saqqara and Giza and entrusted those in Upper Egypt to his assistants. He wanted to concentrate first on the study, *in situ*, of the most ancient monuments: those of the Memphite Empire. 'Ten years ago,' he was to write, in an article dated October 1868, at Saqqara, 'the monuments of the Old Kingdom still had, apart from their own archaeological interest, all the attraction of their novelty. Champollion [the great French scholar who first deciphered hieroglyphs in 1822] and his successors had barely looked at them. Forced to extend all over the place, the Prussian Commission had not necessarily exhausted the subject. Up to a point it was new or little explored and we had, least of all, to neglect it as it was really here that a service could be rendered to science and a void filled.'[20]

Mariette succeeded in having the Egyptologist Théodule Devéria, assistant keeper in the Louvre's Department of Egyptian Antiquities, seconded to him in Egypt. He joined Mariette in late December. In his diaries Devéria makes Mariette live again during those years of 1858 and 1859 when, conscious of the supreme authority delegated to him by the Viceroy in relation to the antiquities, he unrelentingly spent all the energy of his robust constitution.[21] With his infectious enthusiasm, he carried all his assistants along; some of them, however, were unable to stand the strain and one, Bonnefoy, died of exhaustion early in 1859.

It was during 1860 that Mariette made, in the Memphite necropolis, the series of discoveries which were his most important after that of the Serapeum. First, in January, was the discovery of the famous wooden statue, dating from the end of the IVth Dynasty or the beginning of the Vth, of the official Ka-aper (since known as the 'Shekh-el-beled'), whose eyes are inlaid with quartz or crystal set in copper. 'The head, especially, is strikingly alive,' he wrote, 'and the whole body is treated with a deep sense of nature. We certainly do not possess another portrait more real and more alive.'[22] The workmen were strongly impressed by this statue and its close resemblance to the headman of their village, so they dubbed it 'Shekh-el-beled' (the head of the village). An equally well-made female statue, found in the same tomb, was called the 'wife of Shekh-el-beled'.

*Pl. 15*

Soon afterwards, at the bottom of a pit in the paving of one of the pillared rooms of the so-called 'Temple of the Sphinx', at Giza, the magnificent green diorite statue of King Khephren was found. It is one of the finest pieces in the Cairo Museum.

### The Mastaba of Ti

Almost simultaneously, at Saqqara, Mariette discovered the mastaba of Ti, a wealthy nobleman contemporary with Nefer-ir-ka-re and Ni-weser-re, kings of the Vth Dynasty. When the mastaba was cleared, two chambers were revealed: the offerings chamber, in which gifts of food would be placed for the use of the dead man's spirit, or *ka*, the walls being covered with a remarkable series of reliefs; and a completely enclosed oblong chamber, which the workmen called a *serdab* (meaning, in Arabic, a corridor), which contained a very beautiful statue of Ti. This chamber was lit only by such light as filtered through from the offerings chamber via three narrow spy-holes in the dividing wall, on the south side of the offerings chamber. The original statue is now in the Cairo Museum, but a reproduction was placed in the serdab in 1937 and can be viewed by peering through one of the spy-holes.

*Fig. 2*

*Pl. 18*

The reliefs, covering both the inner walls of the offerings chamber and those of the porticoed entrance, still retain traces

*Pls. 16, 17*

31

*Pl. I*

of painting and are considered masterpieces of their kind; mostly depicting scenes of agriculture and crafts, these reliefs give us a great deal of information about daily life in Egypt during the Old Kingdom. On the south wall, near the south-east corner of the offerings chamber, Ti – represented on a large scale – is seated on a chair with legs that terminate in bull's hooves; underneath, his favourite greyhound watches with ears pricked. In his right hand Ti holds a short thong folded twice

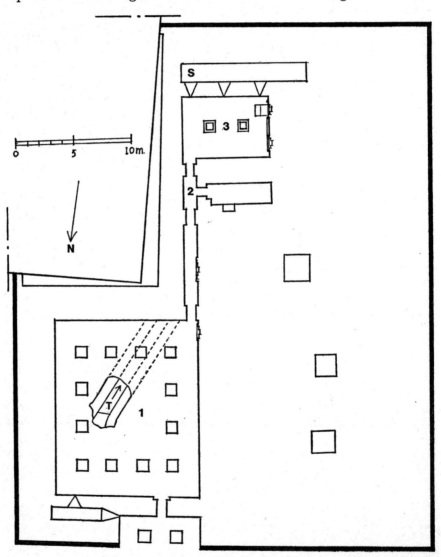

Fig. 2. Plan of the mastaba of Ti, showing: 1, courtyard with subterranean passage (*T*) to inner chambers; 2, passage; 3, offerings chamber with spy-holes to *serdab* (*S*).

1  One of the sphinxes in the avenue leading to the Serapeum; its features appear to be those of Nectanebo I (XXXth Dynasty); height 0·70 m.

2  The semi-circle of poets and philosophers; the statue of Pindar (cf. pl. 4) is the first on the right. In the background are the remains of the *dromos* running westwards to the entrance of the Serapeum.

3  Watercolour, painted at the time of Mariette's excavations, showing the statue of Pindar and another from the semi-circle, as well as sacred animals – lion, panther and two strutting peacocks – all ridden by the young Dionysos, from the *dromos*. Bibliothèque Nationale, Paris.

4  Limestone statue of Pindar. The poet sits majestically on a curved-back chair (imitating a metal one);

the hardness of the seat is apparently offset by a cushion placed on two lion-skins. On the poet's right leg is the top part of a boot resembling a Thracian greave. Height 1·75 m.

5  Strutting peacock amid bunches of grapes; to the left, on the *dromos*, the lion ridden by Dionysos (pl. 8) is partially visible, and to the right the statue of Cerberus (pl. 9) can be seen.

6 Statue of the beneficent deity, Bes; he symbolizes evil overcome, resurrection, fertility and joy, and especially protected women in labour; height 1·00 m. Louvre, Paris.

7 One of the limestone lions found in front of the pylons of the Serapeum's first enclosure. Louvre, Paris.

8  Lion ridden by the young Dionysos; of the child only one of the legs, wearing a Thracian sandal, remains.

9  The statue of Cerberus (with the middle head only remaining), from a photograph taken at the time of Mariette's excavations. This statue is also ridden by the young Dionysos (badly mutilated); note the bunches of grapes under the monster's feet and its tail terminating in a snake's head.

10 An Apis bull; limestone statue discovered in its sanctuary on the *dromos*; height 1·28 m. Louvre, Paris.

11 View of the great torch-lit gallery of the Serapeum (after an engraving published by Arthur Rhoné); to the right is Mariette and, centre, his assistant Devéria.

12  One of the Apis sarcophagi in the Serapeum; made of highly polished black granite, this is one of only two examples that are decorated and inscribed.

*Opposite*
13  Gold pectoral in the form of a flying hawk with a ram's head, found in the tomb of Prince Kha-em-wase in the Serapeum. The cloisonné inlay is made of semi-precious coloured stones; width 0·09 m. Louvre, Paris.

14  Gold *naos*-shaped pectoral, inlaid with coloured glass; found in the wooden sarcophagus of one of the Apis bulls in the Serapeum, it bears the prenomen cartouche of Ramesses II; height 0·13 m. Louvre, Paris.

16, 17 THE MASTABA OF TI: PORTICOED
COURTYARD

*Opposite*
15 The Shekh-el-beled, wooden (probably sycamore) statue of Ka-aper; end of the IVth Dynasty. The lower legs and feet had rotted and have been restored. The staff held in the left hand is not original; the sceptre, once held in the right hand, is lost. The startling realism of the features reveals this as one of the most faithful portraits known of an ancient Egyptian official; height 1·10 m. Cairo Museum.

16 Relief on the west wall: a particularly harmoniously composed group of pigeons.
17 West panel: storks being forcibly fed; the birds are held by the neck while food is inserted into their beaks. Above, to the left, a cook fans the flames with one hand and, with the other, stirs the pot containing the mixture being prepared; near him, to the right, assistants are rolling the food into pellets in their hands.

18  The mastaba of Ti: the statue of Ti (a cast taken from the original now in the Cairo Museum) as seen in the *serdab* through the spy-hole (see p. 31).

19, 20 THE MASTABA OF TI

19 The offerings chamber, south wall: four registers showing various craftsmen at work (for description see pp. 49, 50).

20 The offerings chamber, centre of north wall: a hippopotamus hunt, with Ti shown standing in his boat among papyrus reeds (for description see pp. 50, 51). In the lower register is part of the line of female offering-bearers.

21, 22 THE MASTABA OF TI

21 The offerings chamber, towards the west end of the north wall: a herd of oxen crossing a ford and, in the lower register, a continuation of the procession of offering-bearers seen in pl. 20 (for description see p. 51).

22 Detail of the procession of offering-bearers from Ti's estates.

23, 24  THE MASTABA OF TI

23  The passage, east panel: transporting one of the statues of Ti on a sledge (see p. 53).
24  The offerings chamber, centre of the south wall (to the right of the second spy-hole):
a herd of oxen and, lower register, a fine flock of cranes (see p. 52).

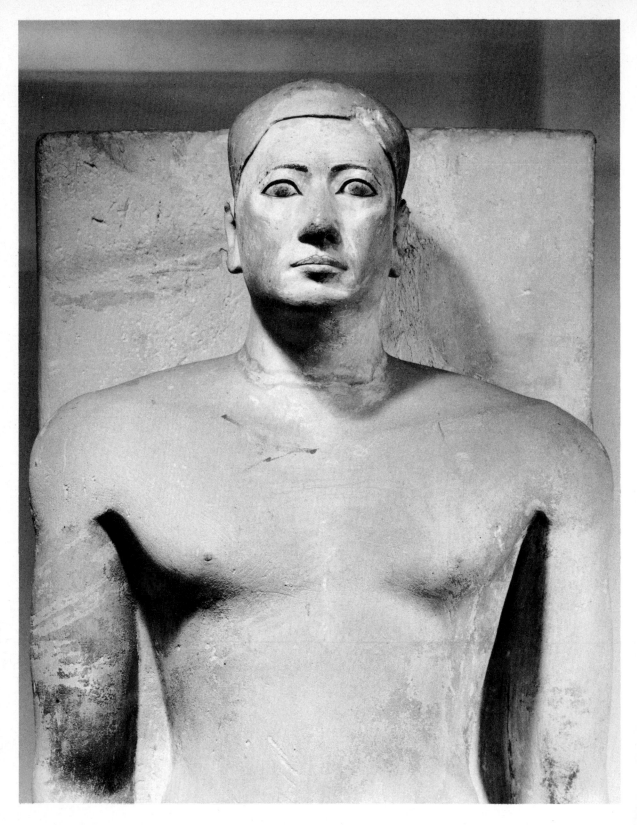

25    Upper half of one of the two life-size statues of Ra-nefer, high priest of the temple of Ptah at Heliopolis (see p. 54); Vth Dynasty. Cairo Museum.

26, 27  Two of the panels found in niches in the west wall of the mastaba of Hesy-re (see pp. 54–5); IIIrd Dynasty. Height 1·50 m. Cairo Museum.

28 The Seated Scribe, Vth Dynasty (see p. 56). The skin is orange-brown and the hair black; the eyes, outlined in oxidized copper, have irises made of rock crystal, the pupils of bronze and the whites of alabaster. Height 0·50 m. Cairo Museum.

29 The Squatting Scribe, Vth Dynasty. Discovered by Auguste Mariette in 1850 (see p. 23), the painted limestone statue has eyes outlined in copper and inlaid with white quartz to form the corneas, rock crystal for the irises and ebony for the pupils. Height 0·55 m. Louvre, Paris.

around his thumb and, in his left, his long staff. His wife – on a much smaller scale – is sitting on the floor with her legs drawn up beneath her; in an affectionate gesture she clasps her husband's left leg with her right arm. These portraits are placed above the first spy-hole from the left, which is flanked by two *ka* priests who offer incense to the statue of Ti within.

Ti and his wife are in fact presiding over the work of various craftsmen, shown in four superimposed registers on the south wall. The upper register, whose left side is lost, concerns the work of goldsmiths. Two of these have partly disappeared, and two others, well preserved, are shown blowing into long blow-pipes to kindle the furnace in which a lump of precious metal is being melted. Nearby a workman is pouring molten metal into an ingot-mould where it will cool, and then be hammered, an operation that is being carried out by two men seated face to face, each with an upraised arm holding a stone hammer; one of the workmen, while shaping the metal ingot on an anvil in front of their knees, says to the other, in the inscription above the scene: 'Give this lump to be baked; it is hardened!'[23]

*Pl. 19*

The register below this relates to sculptors and, on its right-hand edge, makers of stone vases. The part of the sculptors' studio to the left has disappeared except for the legs of the sculptors and their statues, but it is still possible to see that, in addition to the four completed statues, work is proceeding on four others. The sculptors, according to the level at which they have to work on the statues, are shown either standing, sitting on a stool or crouched with one knee on the ground. One notices that, for working on wooden statues, they use not only hammer and chisel but also adzes; for statues in stone, they use mallets made of hardstone, the head being held in a cleft stick, and also polishing stones. To the right of the sculptors' workshop a maker of vases is hollowing out a narrow-necked piece. He is using his *hemti* borer[24] while another, using the same type of tool, is boring out the interior of an almost cylindrical alabaster vase.

In the next register carpenters and cabinet-makers are shown at work. From left to right, a cabinet-maker is polishing a small *naos* (shrine), with torus moulding and a cavetto cornice, immediately above the spy-hole adjoining the knee of Ti's wife. Behind the cabinet-maker two carpenters are polishing a thick piece of wood; then a crouching man shapes a longer piece with his adze while another man, standing up, is sawing lengthwise a post driven vertically into the ground (see also the shipyard scene, Plate IV). Beyond, two seated men are working. One uses a hammer and chisel to cut mortises and the other is sawing. Then come two more cabinet-makers polishing a bed made of ebony (noted in the hieroglyphic caption above them); beneath the bed are a head-rest and a small chest. Lastly, on the right-hand edge, crouches a man with a bow-drill making holes in a chest.[25]

In the lower register, just behind the censer-bearer to the right of the spy-hole, two workmen are straightening canes with the aid of a strong forked bar. The head of the bar is set against a post driven vertically into the ground, and the other end rests on the floor. The two arms of the fork are strongly tied with rope, and one of the men has introduced into the triangle thus formed the end of a long cane, to be straightened or bent as required. The other man puts his lever just below the fork; the first workman then places the portion of the cane to be straightened across the lever, and bears down on it with all his weight by sitting on the other end of the cane.[26]

After this workshop we find that of the tanner who is rubbing some soft material – it can only be a skin – over the top of a tripod. Behind him another craftsman, seated on a small papyrus mat and with his bag of tools under his arm, is a maker of cylinder seals; he appears to be trying to perforate with a punch the seal which is largely hidden by his arm and knees. This work seems to interest a man who is holding the shoulder strap of his bag with one hand, and has in the other a cylinder and a bunch of cords with knotted ends.

Several market scenes follow all this: two men move towards a sandal merchant; one of them, with a load on one shoulder and a bag hanging on the other, proffers a vase in his left hand; but the man in front of him seems to have met with better success, exchanging a mysterious triangular package for the desired pair of sandals. To the right of this group, three traders are going towards a buyer who moves to meet them; he is most interested in the walking stick that the first trader draws from a sheath while saying: 'Here is a very beautiful cane, my friend! A measure of wheat for it!', and the customer replies: 'How I like its head!',[27] presumably meaning its knob.

*Pl. 20*

On the centre of the north wall of the offerings chamber is a classic representation of a hippopotamus hunt. Ti, standing in his boat among the papyrus reeds, is shown on a much larger scale than his boatmen who are harpooning the hippopotami. A hippopotamus has seized a crocodile which, meanwhile, is desperately trying to bite the hippo's leg; behind the hippopotami, fine Nile fish of different species are shown nearly as large, particularly the first, which can be recognized as a *Tilapia nilotica*. Against the stern of Ti's boat is a small papyrus skiff with its stern post curiously truncated. In it is a fisherman, sitting on a low stool of reeds, who has caught a large schal fish (*Synodontis schal*) on the line held in his left hand; he has a club ready in the other. Above Ti, among the papyrus clusters, birds of all sorts have their nests and are being attacked by two genets to the right and a mongoose to the left; the papyrus reeds bend under the weight of these carnivorous animals.

In the lower register are some of the well-known and elegant female bearers laden with produce from Ti's various domains for stocking his tomb. They wear long transparent dresses whose colours, originally alternately varied, have nearly completely disappeared. All these bearers differ slightly from each other, either by the position of their arms, or by the objects they carry in their hands or on their heads.

This long procession of offering-bearers is continued in the lower register at the west end of the wall. Above it is a scene showing a herd of magnificent oxen with lyre-shaped horns preceded by two hornless cows and a calf crossing a ford. The calf, tied to a rope and pulled forward by one of the herdsmen who are in two papyrus boats flanking the herd, forces its mother to follow, thus drawing along the other beasts. An overseer, his hand resting on the head of his long staff of office, is watching the operation from the bank; he calls to the herdsmen: 'Hey, cow-herd! Your hand on the water!' (meaning 'Make the sign of protection' against the crocodiles that can be seen lurking on the bottom, lying in wait for their prey). One of the herdsmen in the right-hand boat, actually makes the required sign, but another man, in the left-hand boat, turns to the overseer and says: 'Don't multiply the voice!'[28]

*Pl. 21*

In the upper register a cow is in labour, helped by the cow-herd, who has grasped the front legs of the calf being born, while an overseer, stretching out his arm with fist closed except for the thumb and index finger, seems to be making a sign to ward off the evil eye.[29] This scene clearly shows the suffering of the mother giving birth, with its head stretched forward with tongue extended; it is a strikingly realistic rendering. Behind, calves are tied, each by a leg, within reach of tufts of grass or plants on which they browse, while two other younger animals flank a cow which has been hobbled in order to be milked, and thus wean the calves; a herdsman holds one of these young animals by its front legs and it turns towards its mother with its tongue out. The natural attitudes of these young animals show remarkable powers of observation on the part of the sculptor of these scenes.

*Pl. II*

Also on the north wall, above the entrance, is a scene showing a small herd of four oxen, with fine lyre-shaped horns, preceded by three hornless cows, still nicely coloured in red ochre, crossing a ford. They follow one of the herdsmen carrying a young calf on his shoulders; it looks back anxiously at its mother, who, with outstretched muzzle, tries to reach it. The legs of the herdsmen and those of the animals, outlined through the zigzag lines which are the conventional way of indicating water, are particularly pleasing and the whole scene is a minor masterpiece of its kind. In the register above herdsmen drive a flock of rams.

*Pl. 24*

More animals and birds are represented in the centre of the south wall of the offerings chamber, immediately to the right of the second spy-hole of the *serdab*. The two upper registers are filled with a line of magnificent oxen, mostly with large lyre-shaped horns. Their muzzles and paunches are beautifully drawn and modelled. They are all wearing collars, some of which are adorned with a large pendant and others with a kind of bell. Herdsmen lead several of the oxen by reins, the others follow docilely.

In the lower register a very fine flock of cranes of different varieties, whose names are carved above several of the birds, is flanked by two men who are herding them by touching their feet with poles. One cannot help but admire the skill with which the artist has so harmoniously arranged the heads and beaks of these long-legged birds, as well as their feet and tufted tails. Also remarkable is the delicate carving of the feathers.

*Pl. III*

On the northern half of the east wall of the offerings chamber we see harvest scenes in the presence of Ti and his wife, who sits at his feet. In the upper register wheat is being harvested using long-handled sickles that cut the stalks at mid-height. Towards the left, a flute-player is entertaining the harvesters and one of these, holding his sickle under his arm, is beating time by clapping. Underneath, some donkeys, driven by their donkey-boys wielding sticks, are taken to be loaded with sheaves of wheat or barley that are being put into large bags made of netting. To the left, with very expressive arm and leg movements, two men are vigorously tying up one of these bags. Beneath these men a stubborn donkey is being beaten and pulled by its leg and ears while another, more docile, animal is allowing itself to be laden normally. Other donkeys preceded by a foal and flanked by their drovers go off carrying large sacks. Further down, the sacks are being untied to form temporary stacks by throwing the sheaves one on top of the other. Further down still, two herds of oxen and donkeys are trampling the sheaves on the threshing floor. Finally, in the bottom register, women are sifting and winnowing the grain with small sweepers and scoops, while chattering together. One of them, to the left of the picture, noticing that her neighbour's sweeping is of little use, tells her: 'Leave this barley, it is husked,' and the other replies: 'I do as you say.'[30] Further to the right, men armed with large wooden three-pronged forks are carefully building conical stacks with the chopped and picked hay, the tops of which they tie with papyrus reeds whose umbels are showing. In the midst of these men, two women are still gleaning some grains using scoops and a sieve.

On the southern half of the east wall we see the shipyard; scenes showing the method of assembly and building a ship,[31] starting from a tree-trunk, which carpenters are shaping on the left. To the right in the first register at the bottom, two workmen are seen astride a large piece of wood placed horizontally on two forked trestles; each man is armed with a mallet and chisel which they are using to cut two mortises in the upper face of the wood while, behind them, another man is busy sawing length-wise a long post driven vertically into the ground and tightened at the top by a cord and a counterweighted lever. Among all the activity depicted here, axes, adzes and large double-headed sledge-hammers are seen in use.

*Pl. IV*

Another very interesting relief occurs on the eastern panel of the passage. It shows one of the statues of Ti being transported on a sledge. The sledge and the statue are shown as normal in profile, while the *naos* containing the statue is shown facing with the two doors open so that the statue can be seen. This is an example of the graphic conventions applied by the ancient Egyptians in order to show each being or object in its most complete or significant aspect. A team of seven men are drawing the sledge while repeating: 'A fine procession!' An eighth man is specially detailed to pour water beneath the runners so that they may better slide on the wet clay-like soil.

*Pl. 23*

Mariette noticed that in most of the mastabas there was a *serdab* similar to the one containing the statue of Ti, and that they likewise often contained statues. He therefore decided to forestall the antiquity shop suppliers by clearing the *serdabs* and removing the very realistic and expressive portraits of officials and notables of the Old Kingdom which they contained. They were to populate the projected museum of antiquities in Cairo.

*Pl. 25*

In March, 1860, Mariette wrote a letter to the Keeper of the Louvre, Emmanuel de Rougé, telling him of the discovery at Saqqara of a score of these statues and particularly of one of two life-sized figures of Ra-nefer, high-priest of the temple of Ptah at Heliopolis during the Vth Dynasty.[32] In one of the statues he is shown wearing a half-length wig; concerning the second, in which the short-cropped hair is painted black and the body orange-red, Mariette added: 'The neck, the pectoral muscles, the arms, the legs – everything is very vigorous and reveals the artist who, without infringing the sacred laws mentioned by Plato, allows himself to be carried away by a sound imitation of nature. The head, also, is a portrait, and to see those eyes, that look, and that mouth as if about to speak, one could believe the statue alive . . .'[33] The statue is now in the Cairo Museum.

One evening, during that most fruitful winter of 1860, while Mariette was walking about the necropolis looking for new sites to dig, he saw, rising from the ruins of a tomb ravaged long before, a stone fragment carved with the cartouche of a king of one of the early dynasties. An immediate excavation revealed other royal cartouches, several of which were then unknown, and, eventually, a whole list of kings being worshipped by the owner of the tomb, a scribe called Tjuneroy who was a contemporary of Ramesses II. These cartouches proved to be the famous 'Table of Saqqara' enumerating among others, fifty-seven cartouches of some of the most ancient kings, and thus a valuable document for the reconstitution of the early dynasties. Also at Saqqara, a few years later, Mariette discovered two magnificent alabaster tables, decorated with the heads and paws of lions, which are now in the Cairo Museum.[34] They were found in one of the archaic tombs within the Step Pyramid complex.

*Pls. 26, 27*

It was at this time that he uncovered the important mastabas of Hesy-re and Kha-bau-Soker, both of the IIIrd Dynasty. Hesy-re lived during the time of King Zoser, the builder of the Step Pyramid. Some remarkable carved wooden panels, two of the best preserved of which are illustrated, were part of the lining of six of the eleven niches in the mud brick western wall of the passage of Hesy-re's mastaba.[35]

On one panel, Hesy-re is shown seated at a stool with bull's-feet legs in front of his table of offerings, above which are hieroglyphs that list the food. Wearing a curled wig and a long tight-fitting robe fastened on the left shoulder by a buckle leaving the right shoulder and arm completely free, he stretches out his hand towards the table. His scribe's kit is thrown over his shoulder and he holds his staff in his left hand, and also what appears to be the symbol of his authority, his *kherep* sceptre. Above his head the upper part of the panel is taken up by his name and the list of his titles and functions.

On the other panel, Hesy-re is shown walking, his *kherep* sceptre in his right hand, his long staff and his scribe's kit is to his left. He is wearing a long wig and the official pleated loin cloth. His effigy is similarly surmounted by his name and titles, but in shorter form than on the preceding panel.

Mariette, therefore, examined a considerable number of mastabas, sometimes only superficially in order to remove the statues they contained. He copied the inscriptions and drew plans of 115 of them and was able to publish, in the *Revue Archéologique* of January 1869, an article entitled 'Sur les tombes de l'Ancien Empire que l'on trouve à Sakkara'. But it was only after Mariette's death that Gaston Maspero published, in January 1881, the descriptive work on these tombs entitled *Mastabas de l'Ancien Empire*.

# III

## New Discoveries Made by Mariette's Successors, 1881–1931

In 1881 Maspero, who had just discovered, inside the ruined pyramids of the VIth Dynasty Kings Pepi I and Merenre at Saqqara, the very important magico-religious hieroglyphs since known as the 'Pyramid Texts' (see Chapter IX), naturally concentrated his explorations, no more on the mastabas, but on the pyramids of the VIth Dynasty and of the period immediately preceding it. A dozen years passed, and it was only in the summer of 1893 that excavations carried out by Jacques de Morgan (who had just replaced Grébault as head of the Antiquities Department, Maspero having left for France to resume his teaching at the Collège de France and the Ecole des Hautes Etudes) uncovered the beautiful statue of an anonymous scribe, known as the Seated Scribe of the Cairo Museum, and several most important mastabas. These were at Saqqara, just to the north of the pyramid of Teti, the adjoining mastabas of Mereruka (also called Mera or Mery) and Kagemni; and, a few kilometres away at Abusir, the mastaba of Ptah-shepses, vizier and son of King Sahu-re of the Vth Dynasty. But de Morgan did not complete the clearing of this last mastaba, preferring to go to Dahshur to explore the two mud-brick pyramids of the Middle Kingdom, which led him to the discovery of the magnificent jewels belonging to the queens and princesses of the XIIth Dynasty.[36]

### The Mastaba of Mereruka

The very large mastaba of Mereruka, unusually, included a large section reserved for his wife, the Princess Har-watet-khef, who was the daughter of the pharaoh Teti. As in the other mastabas of the period, the scenes carved in the walls are full of lively interest and great detail. In Room 1 the north wall has a very fine scene of hunting in papyrus marshes. A detail from it, in front of Mereruka's large reed boat, shows the many different types of bird that have nested or are simply perching in the papyrus thicket. A man standing in the prow of a small boat propelled by four punters holds the tail of a large mongoose

*Pl. 28*

*Fig. 3*

*Pl. 31*

trained to hunt. It climbs up a papyrus stalk that bends beneath its weight, trying to reach a nest full of young kingfishers, despite their parent birds who are attacking it with their long beaks. Beneath this nest, a Nile goose sits on its eggs in its nest and, just behind the mongoose, a fine tufted heron is perched on a papyrus cluster. Further away, towards the left, one can see a flamingo perching just beneath a nest in which an ibis sits on its eggs. Lastly, right at the top and to the left, a second mongoose can be seen returning down a papyrus stalk with a fledgling in its mouth.

In the water underneath the two boats, hippopotami and crocodiles are fighting: one of the hippopotami has caught a crocodile by its middle and is about to break its back; in front of them a young hippopotamus is peacefully following some fishes represented much bigger than itself. The one shown completely in the photograph is a Nile perch (*Lates niloticus*).

Also in Room 1, but on the south wall, near the south-east corner, in the bottom register a herd of oxen and cows are de-

*Pl. 32*

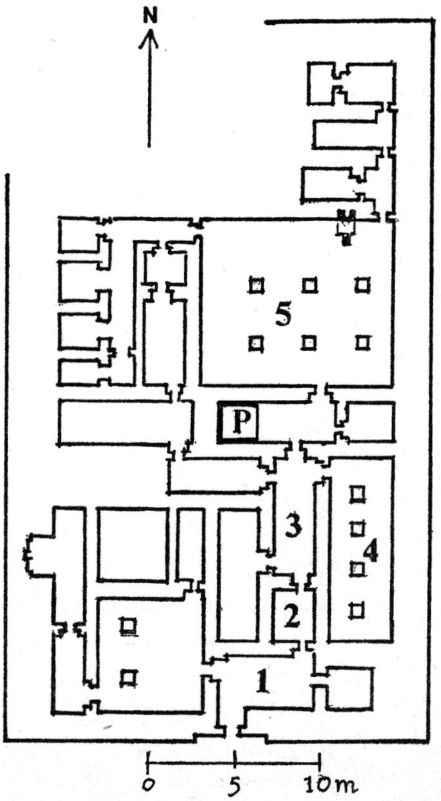

Fig. 3. Plan of the mastaba of Mereruka.

picted swimming across a swamp, flanked by their herdsmen in small papyrus-reed boats, each steered by a single oar. To the left, in the first boat, one of the herdsmen is quietly seated in the prow holding his staff, and another herdsman is dragging a calf through the water by a rope held in both hands; as usual, the cow, whose horns have been cut off, follows its calf, reaching out towards it with its muzzle and tongue, thus drawing along the rest of the herd. Following the herd comes a second boat. The caption in hieroglyphs above the herdsman who kneels on its prow reads: 'Hey, herdsman! Your hand on the water!' (the same phrase occurs in the mastaba of Ti, see p. 51), and he is seen stretching out his arm in a magic gesture to ward off the crocodile shown lying in wait in the water. It is apparently effective, as the crocodile seems to be immobile.

The second register shows a particularly animated scene of men trying to bring down sacrificial oxen. From left to right one sees a man leaping over the back of the first ox. He grabs one of its horns with his right hand and has hold of its tail in his left. Three other herdsmen also set upon the unfortunate beast. One swings on the other horn, a second is trying to trip its front legs and the third has flung his arms around its hocks. Two other oxen suffer the same fate but the attitudes of the men are different: one rides astride the second beast's withers, while a herdsman balances on the third beast's rump and strains with both his hands and feet on its horns to force the animal to lower its head. Lastly, behind a fourth ox that has just been made to lie down, a man rises on tiptoe and agilely lifts his left leg to press back one of the horns on which he is also heaving with both hands.

The top register is concerned with watering gardens. Under the eye of an overseer preceded by his young son and by a slightly bigger boy carrying a load on his head, gardeners are bringing water in jars carried on shoulder yokes. One of these men, as he reaches the kitchen garden, conventionally shown in the plan by three rows of small rectangles, prepares to pour out one of his jars while another man in front of him has just finished emptying his own. Next, several gardeners, one of whom picks a large fruit that has ripened, are working with dibbles.

*Pl. 33*

In Room 2 scenes on the west wall show hunting in the desert; these are set between two palisades that seem to delimit the area from which the game is being flushed.[37] In the lower register, two large greyhounds pounce, one on an oryx which it bites on the nape of the neck, and the other on an ibex (Nubian bouquetin) which it has knocked over and seized by the throat. A second oryx manages to escape having seen the danger, looking backwards in a beautifully realistic movement. Between the two victims of the hunting dogs, a seated lion is calmly savaging the muzzle of a wild bull that it has seized with its forepaws and the unfortunate victim, in fear and agony, is defecating. Above the larger part of this ferociously animated scene one finds, in contrast, among the tufts of cacti growing in the sand-dunes, two hedgehogs quite normally and naturally emerging from their burrows, a young gazelle lying down and a hare sitting up.

In the upper register a quartered ibex has been thrown to the pack of hounds who are tearing it to pieces. To the right of this scene, a hunter holds the end of a rope with which he seems to have lassoed one of the ibexes or gazelles which can be seen in front of him.

Scenes on the east wall of Room 2 show a great deal of activity. In the upper register two groups of six men are pulling a sled carrying a statue of the deceased in a lightly-built shrine. Two men flank the *naos* in the centre of the photograph: one of them is offering incense to the statue while the other steadies the *naos*. *Pl. 34*

In the centre register goldsmiths are seen at work. To the left an overseer weighs gold ingots on the beamed balance; a scribe notes the number of cubic weights that it takes to balance each ingot. In the centre, six workmen are using long blow-pipes to heat the fire in order to melt the gold ingots in the crucibles. As we saw in Ti's tomb, the molten metal is then poured into a mould where it will be cooled sufficiently to be hammered; we do in fact see, immediately following, men kneeling and sitting on their heels with raised hands, holding a pebble, to 'hammer the gold', written in hieroglyphics above the ingot in front of them, on the anvil.

Both above and below these goldsmiths the principal products of their art are displayed: slender vases with or without spouts, ewers and basins, various necklaces, a diadem etc. Finally, in the lower register, workmen, mostly rather fat or dwarfs, are putting the finishing touches to various kinds of necklaces. According to the hieroglyphic captions cut above the two groups of small dwarfs, one of them, especially satisfied with their handiwork, a long necklace bigger than themselves, is exclaiming: 'It is beautiful, comrade!' But another, on the con-

*Pl. 35*

*Pl. V*

*Pl. 37*

trary, is chivvying his friend who is still working hard with his bodkin to finish the piece, saying: 'Hurry up, finish it!'[38]

The law-court scene on the west wall of Room 3 has been damaged and all one can see of the judge, situated on the left, is one hand holding a roll of papyrus, and the bottom part of one of his legs. In front of him the clerk's office has two lotiform columns. Behind the clerks the first three accused, farmers, are kneeling with arms folded and bent forward in an attitude of submission. Others following are dragged or pushed forward by guards who are free with the use of their sticks; lastly, towards the right-hand edge, a convicted man, completely naked, is held across a post by one of the guards while two others beat him with rods.

The principal room of the mastaba was the Room of Pillars (Room 5), into which Mereruka's *ka* statue, attached to the rear wall of its niche, steps with startling realism through his false door in the north wall. On each side of the statue's niche, on the frame, his names and titles are engraved. As with stelae, the sides of the niche are edged by a vertical, beribboned torus moulding, and at the foot of the niche an offerings table is preceded by four steps. On the wall on each side, Mereruka is shown in relief walking away from the niche; in both cases he is preceded by his wife wearing on her head a ribbon diadem and smelling a lotus flower, and is followed by his mother, both women being shown below the level of the bottom of his kilt. Beneath these figures the black paint of the dado, as well as the two bands in yellow and red which separate it from scenes in relief, are especially well preserved.

Very interesting scenes occur on the north wall, to the right of the statue, above the doorway to the passage leading north. Here we see adolescent games; young men, on the upper two registers, and young women in the register over the lintels. The young men are wearing the side-lock of youth and are nude. On the first register, starting at the top, from left to right, a young boy balances on all fours on the horizontally outstretched arms of a bigger boy who is supported by two other young men, one on each side. Then, a trial of strength between two groups of three boys in a sort of tug-of-war; the file leaders are holding hands and pulling by throwing themselves vigorously backward, each trying to draw the other towards him. Lastly, to the right, is a game of *khazza lawizza*:[40] the two seated boys, arms and legs stretched forward, are represented here, by artistic convention, one above the other; they should, in reality, be represented face to face forming an obstacle to be vaulted over by the three boys running towards them.

On the next register is a kind of war game;[41] the enemy, shown as a prisoner with his arms tied behind his back, is led at a jog-trot by the other boys; further away, to the right, he has fallen to his knees and is being heavily kicked by the others. Beneath this, four girls are playing a game;[42] two of them, back to back and with legs slightly apart, act as a pivot around which their two partners rapidly turn by holding their hands and leaning stiffly backwards. Then a group of four girls perform the 'mirror dance'.[43] Finally, lower still, to the right of the doorway, a young man is carrying, on his right forearm supported by his left hand, a much smaller boy who is balancing himself in order to stay upright.

Also on the north wall of the Room of Pillars, but to the left of the statue, are curious scenes showing animals being forcibly fed. On the upper register four *Oundjou* antelopes or goats with long twisted horns are lying before their respective shepherds who, in order to feed them, are either simply holding them by the snout or by a lead tied to a collar.

*Pl. VI*

Below it is a psssing herd of very fine *Ioua* oxen with lyre-shaped horns, led by their herdsmen; the leading ox, which lowers its head towards a bale of hay, has a crooked horn. An extremely fat ox which is hornless brings up the rear.

In the third register all the oxen are lying down except for the last one, which has a pair of exceptionally well-developed horns, and is kneeling in order to drink more easily from a large jar held by the herdsman. Three other herdsmen, each sitting in front of his ox that he holds by a leash, have each thrust a hand and part of the forearm into the beast's mouth in order to feed it hay by the handful.

In the second register from the bottom, different animals including several kinds of antelope (an oryx, a spotted-nose addax, a brown addax, a Nubian goat and a dorcas gazelle) are shown tethered next to their mangers.

In the lower register, we witness the extraordinary operation of force-feeding hyenas (also depicted in the mastaba of Kagemni, Pl. 49). The beast, tightly held and led by two attendants, arrives flat-bellied; after it has been turned over on its back, one of the men holds its paws, tied if necessary, while the other pushes meat into its mouth; after this operation is completed the beast goes off, its stomach now well rounded, still flanked by two attendants. It is possible that this procedure is connected

*Pl. 38*

with animals being trained for hunting; as a result of force-feeding, they would lose the incentive to devour their prey.[44]

On the west wall, large sailing boats are depicted under full sail, with two-legged crane-masts,[45] pushed by the north wind; they pass in front of Mereruka who is waiting for them with his wife sitting at his feet. To the left the tip of Mereruka's foot can be seen, and also his wife's knees, and one of her bent arms with the stem of the lotus flower she is holding.

In the first boat, the oarsmen, seated at their posts, have lifted their oars and two boatswains are in the prows;[46] however, as neither of them is carrying the usual boat-hook, one can only suppose that the boat is not going to stop there. In the stern, the helmsman is holding the two long oars that serve as the rudder, while the man in charge of the sail, sitting on his high platform, is working the sail by means of two lines leading to the edges of the yard arm, upon which a small monkey is cavorting. Other sailors stand holding on to the shrouds with one hand.

The second boat is following the first so closely that the boatswain in the bows has been able to take hold of the first boat's stern, probably to ward it off. The oarsmen have left their oars and, under the watchful eye of a quartermaster, are working the halyards.

*Pl. 39*

On the south wall to the east of the entrance passage, among the papyrus reeds beneath the prow of Mery's boat, a fine swimming otter has just caught a mullet (*Mugil capito*) which it holds in its claws while avidly devouring it. Just underneath, a crocodile, lurking on the bottom, faces a large fish (*Lates*), about to be harpooned, and which is followed by another fish (*Tilapia*), itself in similar danger of being harpooned.

*Pl. 40*

Lastly, on the east wall, northern edge, Mery with his wife behind him holding a lotus flower (both unfortunately truncated) are sitting on a couch with lions'-paw legs; Mery is playing a game of *zenet*,[47] a kind of draughts, with his smaller opponent. Each has a piece in his hand. Behind them, and in the lower register, bearers present various offerings watched by overseers who make signs of acceptance and thanks.

To the left, off Room 1, part of the mastaba was reserved for Mereruka's wife – the daughter of Teti, the princess Har-watet-khet, whose 'beautiful' name is Seshseshet. In Room 6, on the far left, is a false door decorated with panelling; notice here the representations in relief of the hinges and of the planks of the door panel. To the right, the princess is seated on a chair with the usual lions'-paw legs and in front of the traditional table

*Pl. 42*

towards which she stretches out her right hand, while she in-
hales the scent of a lotus flower held in her left hand. She wears
a simple diadem on her head, the so-called 'boatman's circlet',
knotted at the back and having long trailing ribbons. On the
lower register, bearers are presenting the legs of butchered
cattle sacrificed to her and some large geese.

### The Mastaba of Kagemni

This mastaba adjoins that of Mereruka and is also of the VIth    *Fig. 4*
Dynasty. Kagemni too was a vizier and had the walls of his
tomb decorated with the now familiar scenes of daily life. The
workmanship is very fine and this can be seen especially in those
scenes that are essentially minor ones, compared with the large
representations of the tomb's owner. On the east wall of Room
2, for example, five dancers are depicted performing a frenzied    *Pl. 43*
ballet that seems to defy the laws of gravity.[48] On the northern
wall to the left of the passage in Room 2 is a scene showing
Kagemni in his boat. To the right of the stern of the vizier's    *Pl. 44*
boat, three men are in a small papyrus skiff with raised poop;
while one of them, kneeling in the stern, guides it with a boat-
hook, the other two are fishing, one with a net and the other
with a multi-hooked line. A schal fish has been caught on one

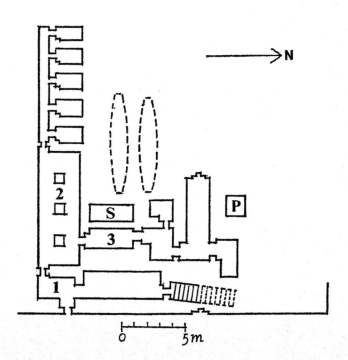

Fig. 4. Plan of
the mastaba of
Kagemni.

I, II

THE MASTABA OF TI

I   The offerings chamber, south wall near the south-east corner. Ti, represented on a large scale, and his wife are seen presiding over the work of
craftsmen (cf. Plate 19 and pp. 32, 49, 50).

II   The offerings chamber, north wall, above the entrance (cf. p. 52). A
small herd of oxen with fine lyre-shaped horns, preceded by three hornless
cows, are shown crossing a ford. They are following one of the herdsmen who
carries a calf on his shoulders; it looks back towards its mother which, with
outstretched muzzle, tries to reach it. The legs of the herdsmen and of the
animals, seen outlined through the water (shown in the conventional way as
a series of zig-zag lines), are especially pleasing.

I

II

III

IV

III, IV

of the hooks, and a large Nile perch is about to be hooked. To the left of the net, where a mullet, swimming between two lotus flowers will probably soon be caught, crocodiles are mating. Directly above them, one can see, at the end of the stem of an aquatic plant (*Potamogeton lucens*)[49] a dragonfly and a frog and, higher up, on another stem, a large grasshopper.

*Pl. 45*

Near the west end of this wall are scenes of cattle. On the lower register a herd of oxen with wide lyre-shaped horns and muzzles modelled in remarkably fine relief, are preceded by two hornless cows, and crossing a stretch of water. One of the cow-herds in a papyrus boat holds a calf by a lead and its front hooves: it looks anxiously back at its mother which tries to reach the tip of its tail with its tongue; the mother draws along the rest of the herd, one of which has already started to turn back. Two other cow-herds, crossing on foot, bring up the rear, one of them drives the herd forward with a stick and the other carries on his back a second calf, its head turned backwards as it extends its tongue, apparently out of fear. Beneath the herd, various types of fish are swimming, a young hippopotamus stands in the water and a crocodile prepares to snap up a large fish.

In the upper register, a cow is being milked. It has been immobilized by a rope tightly wound around the upper part of its hind legs and tied to its horns, while a third cow-herd chases away its calf by lashing it with a rope. Another cow to the right, however, is suckling its young calf; here the cow-herd has hobbled the cow's hind legs by means of a rope that passes over its back to one of its front legs which is thus lifted and bent.

*Pl. 47*

In Room 3, on the north wall, Kagemni, whose name and several titles (which included those of vizier and minister of justice) are inscribed above his left shoulder and arm, is sitting in his carrying chair holding a short cane which is curiously passed through his fingers. He is being carried by a score of men, each holding a baton, placed in two ranks of ten separated by an officer; behind and in front of these bearers, two attendants hold the long handles of his sun shades. Lastly, the monkey and the dogs held on leads by a dwarf are not, as in Mereruka's tomb, under their master's chair between the two files of bearers, but here, because of lack of space on this narrow panel, are relegated to the lower register just above the door lintel.

*Pl. 48*

Several of the other scenes in Room 3 are concerned with birds. On the southern half of the west wall, in the bottom register, is a scene depicting bird-hunting with a net. From left to right, four men run to the right and look backwards to the net that they are pulling into position; the last man raises his left hand, doubtless to silence his companions. In front of them another net has just been dropped (at the signal of a hunter shown standing with arms outstretched) upon a flock of geese and wild duck sitting on the surface of a pond ringed by water plants, mostly blue and white lotus. Above, several birds which have escaped the net fly off; below, drawn and sculpted with wonderful fineness and observation, are small waders, the first of which, a heron egret, holds a fish in its beak; they, however, do not seem in the least perturbed. Notice, between the pond and the hunter with the outstretched arms, the thick post to which the cord of the net was tied.

The second register shows an aviary in which numerous ducks and geese are pecking, with astonishing realism, at the grain that has just been thrown to them by a farmhand. The aviary is surrounded by forked posts that are joined to each other at the top by a drawn cord, and which must have carried the nets. Its entrance was decorated with small columns having capitals made of open lotus flowers, only one of which now remains, to the right of the scene. The structure of the aviary is shown in elevation, and is divided into several adjoining enclosures strewn with grain and each having, in the centre, a rectangular basin with diagonal channels going from each corner towards the exterior. The basins, however, are seen from above. These last details, shown thus in plan, are lifted to the vertical, as in descriptive geometry – the usual practice in Egyptian reliefs.

In the top register, which is broken off, breeders are forcibly feeding geese by pushing specially prepared balls of food, set out on trays, into their beaks. Another very realistic scene of geese being forcibly fed appears on the northern part of the west wall. The artist proves, by the various realistic and natural attitudes chosen for each of these birds, that he is an exceptionally gifted portrayer of fowl. No less remarkable are the precise gestures of each breeder skilfully holding the head of a goose in order to force into its beak, with his thumb and forefinger, one of the balls of food that his helper, seated in front of him, is preparing by rolling them between his hands and piling them on a tray.

*Pl. 49*

In the top register, hyenas are shown being forcibly fed, in a scene similar to the one in the tomb of Mereruka (cf. p. 61).

De Morgan's successor, Victor Loret, concentrated on the site north of the pyramid of the VIth Dynasty king, Teti. There

*Fig. 5*

*Pls. 50, 51*

*Pl. 52*

*Pl. 53*
*Pl. 54*

he discovered, between July 1897 and February 1898, the funerary temples of the two small pyramids of the queens Iput and Khuit – the former, at least, being the wife of Teti – and also what has been called the 'Street of Tombs', a narrow street running between several mastabas of the same period.[50]

The most important of these mastabas, that of Ankh-ma-Hor, is known today as the 'Tomb of the Doctor' because of certain scenes represented in its reliefs, such as a toe operation and circumcision. Despite these very individual scenes, there are also examples of the usual daily life genre, such as a panel on the north wall in Room 3 where an oryx and a dorcas gazelle are each led by two men who hold them firmly by the horns. One of the herdsmen also holds, by the tip of its tail, the gazelle which suckles its kid in passing. In the upper register six men, under a foreman, are busy bringing down a magnificent ox with large lyre-shaped horns; this animated scene is made the more amusing by the actions of the two drovers who are holding on to the beast's tail.

On the south wall of Room 2 the scenes on each side of the door show a group of female dancers similar to that seen in the mastaba of Kagemni (Pl. 43), and a procession of dignitaries followed by groups of male and female mourners, among whom

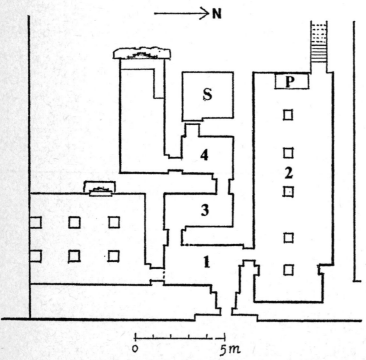

Fig. 5. Plan of the mastaba of Ankh-ma-Hor.

some women are seen fainting. A notable feature in the upper register is the presence of a woman among a procession of dignitaries.

### The Mastaba of Ptah-hotep and Akhet-hotep

During the same period, the Egyptologist N. de G. Davies had been authorized, in 1898, to re-clear the mastaba of Ptah-hotep and Akhet-hotep which Mariette had only superficially described in his *Mastabas* (on p. 359), published by Maspero. This made possible the exhaustive description of this mastaba with its especially remarkable reliefs.[51] Since then, it has been open to visitors and is one of the most frequently visited mastabas.

*Fig. 6*

A relief on the west wall in Room 1 of this mastaba is of particular interest for the latter's titles and from a technical viewpoint. To the right Akhet-hotep, shown standing very large, has above him an inscription giving his name and titles, including those of inspector of the priests of the Vth Dynasty pyramids of the kings Ni-weser-re, Men-kau-hor and Djed-ka-re. Behind him, the damaged upper register shows wheat or barley being reaped with sickles and, immediately underneath, donkey-boys are seen leading away their donkeys with laden panniers.

*Pl. 55*

Of the two registers that should have existed lower down, only the bottom register has been drafted out but not entirely finished; although the small herd of oxen to the right is well modelled, it is not so with the three central herdsmen or with the troop of donkeys which are trampling the ears on the threshing floor. Only their outline has been sketched, except for the lowered head of one of the donkeys, which is trying to snap up a plant.

Room 3, built for Ptah-hotep, has on its wall some of the most important and detailed reliefs in the mastaba, and the high ceiling stones are sculpted to imitate small round logs and are painted in red ochre (a convention to indicate wood in ancient Egyptian monuments). The east wall is particularly animated. In the central part we see an important delivery of fowls and cattle in front of the walking figure of Ptah-hotep; here we can only see the tip of his foot and his hand holding his long stick. He is preceded by his son, Akhti-hotep, shown, like his brother Ptah-hotep, as a child and, like him, holding the bottom of his father's stick with one hand. With the other hand he has a bird by the wings. The lower register involves storks, geese, ducks and pigeons. In the other two registers magnificent oxen are shown; the first one is specially striking for the size of its fine lyre-

*Pl. 56*

*Pl. 57*

shaped horns and for its modelling in relief; a herdsman with a stiff leg, perhaps caused by a horn thrust, leads the animal by a rein. The oxen in the upper register have their horns shown distinctly smaller than usual, indicating, no doubt, that they are of a different breed.

Above a scene of cord-twisting is a very fine representation of a desert hunt which covers two registers. In the first, from left to right, a squatting hunter with two large saluki greyhounds on leads points to a lion savaging the muzzle of a wild bull which, through fear and pain, defecates (compare with the similar scene in Mereruka's tomb, Plate 33). Beyond the lion other hunting dogs have seized an ibex and an oryx by the throat and nape respectively; in front of them a huntsman, chasing after a gazelle and two wild bulls, has succeeded in lassoing one of the latter. The chase continues in the next register which shows, to the left, a greyhound and two hyenas together who seem ready to intervene at the kill of an oryx that has just been pulled down by another greyhound. Next we see an unfortunate gazelle, suckling its kid and, standing behind, a large saluki which has seized an ibex by the thigh; notice the gazelle's action of raising horizontally the attacked hind leg. Lastly, beyond and to the right, two pairs of panthers and wolves are shown mating.

The next register is devoted to the grape harvest. To the left

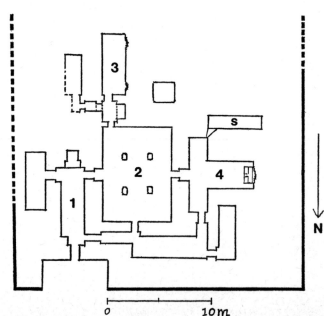

Fig. 6. Plan of the mastaba of Ptah-hotep and Akhet-hotep.

bunches of grapes are gathered from a trellis; then five vintagers are trampling on these bunches while steadying themselves with one hand on a bar; then, to the right, the pressing: a bag containing grapes is twisted as strongly as possible so as to squeeze the juice out into a vat. To do this, the two opposite ends of the bag are each tied round a long stick and these sticks are then turned in opposite directions; in order to maintain the greatest distance between the ends of the two sticks, each pulled by two men, a fifth vintager takes up a really acrobatic position by placing one foot on each stick and bearing down with all his strength on one of them.

In the penultimate register towards the top are shown adolescent games. From left to right a fast game of mock war in which the nomadic enemy, thrown to the ground, is trying to escape the vigorous kicks and blows that rain upon him; next a small group of boys are playing a circling game (see Plate 37, a similar scene in Mereruka's tomb where girls are playing this game), and three big boys are making a smaller boy walk on all fours upon their touching shoulders. A fourth group, playing at *khazza lawizza*, as in Mereruka (see p. 60) precede a boy on all fours carrying on his back two younger boys who are trying to maintain their balance. Finally, to the far right, two youngsters who seem to be duelling, are, in fact, playing at target shooting, a game which consists in throwing pointed sticks from a distance into a circle drawn on the ground.[52] Two sticks already pushed into the ground are crossed in the form of an x.

The topmost register comprises two more scenes, one of cattle crossing a ford following a reed-boat, and the other the gathering of papyrus. This final scene shows two men tying a thick bundle of papyri, then three others going off bent under their loads and, in the middle of these, a fourth lifting his heavy load on to his back.

Continuing the scenes on this wall, but now from the lowest register upwards, we find at the bottom, behind a man who is offering to Ptah-hotep a goose whose beak he holds closed with one hand, boatmen are manœuvring their small reed-boats, laden with various provisions, by means of long poles. Sailing among the lotus plants and over large fish of various kinds, they exchange vigorous blows with their poles from one boat to another.

In the second register wild geese and ducks are being netted. This scene is more condensed than Kagemni's (Plate 48), and the principal events are shown one above the other: below, the

*Pl. 58*

open net with the waiting hunters sitting holding the ropes and, above, the lowered net where at a signal from the chief with outstretched arms who waves a scarf, they heave on the ropes, bending backwards and lying flat on the ground to get more purchase. Behind them two men are caging the captured birds.

In the third register, some workmen finish building papyrus boats. They are mainly busy putting the papyrus bundles in place and tightening the reed ropes: in the picture above, two other workmen are preparing and twisting the cords ready for them.[53]

*Pl. 59*

At the northern end of the east wall is a large-scale portrait of Ptah-hotep. He is shown walking holding his long stick in his right hand and a thong in his left, and preceded by his son, also called Ptah-hotep. The latter, though depicted as quite young with the side-lock of youth, already has the titles of judge and provincial administrator; with one hand he grasps the bottom of his father's stick and in the other holds a hoopoe by its wings.

*Pl. VII*

The central part of the western wall shows Ptah-hotep, wearing a priestly panther skin, seated on a chair with lions'-paw legs before his table. He stretches out his right hand towards it and the food which is heaped around it, and holds a goblet in his left hand just in front of his face. Below the table an inscription in hieroglyphs asserts that a thousand of each of the principal offerings are at his disposal: loaves, jars of beer, alabaster vases, textiles, oxen, poultry and gazelles.

To the right of Ptah-hotep, lines of offering-bearers covering three registers advance towards Ptah-hotep; they stand out from the well-preserved blue-grey background. The first bearer of the top register holds a small bundle of papyrus stalks of a fine green colour under one arm and a libation vase in his hand while presenting a bunch of lotus flowers with the other. The next bearer brings a calf which he carries on his shoulders and, while holding the animal still with his arm around its neck, he manages to carry a basket containing a bunch of lotus flowers in his free hand. The other bearers are carrying various offerings – piled-up trays, poultry, flowers and vegetables; and several are leading some young animals – calf, antelope, ibex, or gazelle.

After Loret's departure the orientation of the excavations was again modified. Maspero, having returned and been re-appointed Director-General, preferred to complete his previous explorations on the inscriptions in the pyramids by the study of the other elements of the complexes that contained them and which he had earlier been obliged to neglect because of lack of funds. With this in mind, he entrusted to Alexandre Barsanti, engineer of the Antiquities Department, in December 1899, the clearing of the approaches to the pyramid of Unas[54] whose fine funerary chamber, covered with these important hieroglyphic texts, was made accessible to tourists.

*Pls. 60, XV*

It was only later, with the appointment of J. E. Quibell as Chief Inspector at Saqqara, that excavations were resumed in the area of Teti's pyramid. But Maspero directed that the dumping of the rubble should be towards the east and the valley beyond, so it is not surprising that no mastabas with reliefs dating from the Old Kingdom were discovered on that side.[55] Besides, from the end of winter 1906, Quibell, during his second campaign, had to transfer his men to the plateau overlooking the access to the necropolis at a point called 'Ras-el-Gisr',[56] where some remains of mud-brick structures had emerged from the sand and were being removed by seekers of *sebakh* (earth from mud-bricks mixed with ancient rubbish used by peasants as fertilizer).

### The Monastery of St Jeremiah

Numerous monks' cells were then recognized; they had on their eastern walls a rounded niche which served as an oratory some-times decorated with a fresco showing Christ, the Virgin and either an archangel or, more probably, the founding Saint. Some of these paintings and numerous Coptic inscriptions (now in the Coptic Museum in Cairo) were proof that this was, as Maspero had suggested, the site of the Monastery of St Jeremiah. Founded at the end of the fifth century AD, it had been destroyed *c.* 960 by the Arabs.

*Pl. 61*
*Pl. 62*

During the three campaigns that Quibell devoted to the clearing of this monastery,[57] working from north to south, he uncovered a courtyard of fine octagonal paving stones, the hospital, the refectory (which is still recognizable), a square-plan chapel with four columns whose bluish marble bases are still visible, and a vast courtyard, today sanded up. Standing in the courtyard were the granite bases of four fallen columns placed around a granite stump which had undoubtedly served as the pedestal of a basin. It was in this courtyard that the curious 'pulpit' flanked by two columns was found (now displayed in the Coptic Museum in Cairo).

*Pl. 63*

The remains of the main church were a little further south; the site was strewn with columns having finely worked capitals,

*Pls. 64–6*

and other carved elements. The best pieces are now in the Coptic Museum. Three other churches of lesser importance were freed of sand but two are now re-buried.

After these important discoveries of Coptic art, Quibell transferred his workmen to the far north of the necropolis and, during two campaigns, from 1910 to 1912, he explored a vast section of the archaic cemetery that covers the plateau to the west and south-west of Abusir village. Some five hundred mud-brick mastabas of the IInd and IIIrd Dynasties, as well as a large tomb with panelled walls dating from the reign of King Djer of the Ist Dynasty, were cleared and provided numerous finds from this very early period.[58]

Quibell then rediscovered, thanks to a workman who, as a youngster, had worked with Mariette, the large IIIrd Dynasty mastaba of Hesy-re, already referred to; the exact location of this tomb was subsequently lost. He completed the clearing that Mariette had only partially started and this yielded a quantity of new material that enabled him to publish details of this important mastaba.[59]

Twenty years later, during the winter of 1930–1, Cecil M. Firth resumed the exploration of this archaic cemetery, uncovering two large panelled tombs in which were found, on clay jar-stoppers, seal-impressions with the name of Udimu, the fifth king of the Ist Dynasty, and a small crystal vase engraved with his name.[60] Firth's premature death in the summer of 1931 interrupted the work and the excavations were not resumed until 1936 by Walter B. Emery and Zaki Y. Saad (see Chapter IV).

Earlier, from 1912 to 1914, Quibell had returned to the site of the pyramid of Teti and resumed excavations around the mastabas of Mereruka and Kagemni. About twenty metres to the west of the former, he reached the mastaba of Kaemhesit, today re-buried, where he found two fine limestone statues of the owner, together with a wooden panel with a remarkable relief of him.[61]

After the First World War, Firth, who had been put in charge of the site of Saqqara, began by re-opening the interrupted excavations at the site of the pyramid of Teti.[62] He extended them considerably, towards the east and north-east, in the areas started by Loret and Quibell. In the latter direction he cleared the funerary shafts of the great mastabas of Mereruka and Kagemni, the largely ruined mastaba of Ikhekhi, and also the entrance passage into the burial chamber of Queen Iput, mother of Pepi I, whose pink-granite stela he found still in place. Finally, at the mouth of the inclined entrance gallery of Teti's pyramid, in the centre of the base of its eastern face, he uncovered the remains of a small offerings chamber. In 1924 he transferred his excavations to the Step Pyramid complex. He made soundings outside its perimeter to find suitable tipping places for the considerable amount of debris that had to be removed. Several large but considerably ruined mastabas, dating from the beginning of the Vth Dynasty, were thus encountered to the west of the enclosures, but it was essentially to the south of this wall that he made other important discoveries in mastabas of the Vth and VIth Dynasties.

### The Mastaba of Ka-irer

The mastabas discovered by Firth included that of Mitri, in which the intact *serdab* yielded a dozen very fine wooden statues,[63] and that of Ka-irer, the walls of which still retain interesting remains of reliefs. Particularly notable is the lower register of the first room, with a scene showing the weighing of ingots around a very curious balance; its vertical post and beam are in the form of a woman with horizontally outstretched arms, but it is not possible to see how the beam could have been articulated. The representation at the base of this balance should be moved a few centimetres to the left, because the block of stone on which it has been carved was accidentally displaced.

*Pl. 68*

To the left of the balance, the chief scribe submits his accounts on a papyrus roll to Ka-irer (whose feet only are visible in the plate). In the upper panel, behind a sculptor sitting on a high stool who is putting the finishing touches to a stone statue, four small dwarfs are seen perched upon tables making necklaces. To their left the overseer gives an unrolled papyrus scroll to his master, who takes it in his hands.

Another scene shows a marsh in which a crocodile – in front of whose jaws fishermen are pulling up a seine net full of large fishes – is in the process of laying its eggs. Behind the crocodile a mullet (*Mugil capito*) is swimming among the leaves and flowers of blue lotus (*Nymphaea coerulea*).

*Pl. 67*

### The Mastaba of Idut

The very remarkable mastaba of Princess Idut,[64] a presumed daughter of King Unas, was found in 1927 during the work to clear the south enclosure wall of King Zoser. Many of the reliefs

*Fig. 7*

*Pl. 70*

still retain traces of colour and are of particular interest. In Room 1, on the north wall to the right of the passage leading into it, the princess (now lost) was depicted on her large boat; in front of her, fishermen in a papyrus skiff are fishing with a dip-net and hooks. A schal fish (*Synodontis schal*) has been hooked while two others, a *Tetrodon fahaka* and a *Tilapia nilotica*, have escaped. Also to be noted, under the edge of the landing net, is

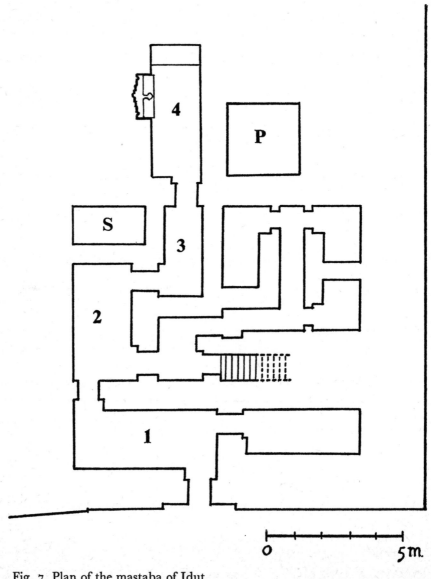

Fig. 7. Plan of the mastaba of Idut.

a *Mormyrus niloticus*, a type that gives the impression of swimming on its back, and, above it, a *Mugil capito* following a Nile perch (*Lates niloticus*).

The fisherman sitting on a low seat in the bow of his boat holds his four-hooked line in one hand and, in the other, a club with which to kill the fish he catches before laying them head to tail in a bag on the prow. Behind him his companion has difficulty in pulling out a net full of fish, from which we see a tiddler jumping to safety; at the stern, only the legs of the steersman have survived.

In Room 2, the main relief on the western wall shows the princess, standing in her boat, watching a hippopotamus hunt. *Pl. 72* In front of her are a fisherman, who dips his net from the shore, and a huntsman who is holding aloft a barbed harpoon, ready to strike again a hippopotamus that he has already harpooned and which is screaming with its companion in the water. Behind this pair of hippos a female gives birth in terror to the great satisfaction of a crocodile who makes ready to devour the new-born baby (see detail, Plate 73). Beyond the crocodile is the same fishing scene represented on Plate 70.

To the left, above the hippopotamus hunter, two animals, a mongoose and a genet, climb up the papyrus thickets towards birds' nests. We may note, from the bottom upwards: a small white heron perched on a papyrus flower; a Nile goose (*Chenalopex aegyptiaca*) and a turtle dove sitting on their nests; then, above the goose, a butterfly between two perched birds; a plover (*Pluvianus aegyptus*) to the right and a whistling duck (*Anas penelope*) standing on one leg. On each side of the mongoose a goose and an ibis (*Ibis aethiopica*), sitting on their nests, flap their wings to frighten away the intruders. Further up, the genet has succeeded in capturing a young bird from a well-stocked nest above which the parents (Nile geese) are diving to try to make it abandon its prey. Behind the genet is a nest of kingfishers (*Ceryle rudis*) with the mother making a protective sortie.

On the large boat, behind the princess, is her nurse Nebet shown on a very small scale in front of a scribe's palette laid on a chest. On shore, finally, an escort of nineteen men, only fifteen of whom are visible here, and each with his title inscribed above his head, are walking towards the princess in various attitudes of deference. The one who, on the lower register, is leading the way, bears the title of '*Ka*-priest of the pharaoh' and has his name engraved in front of his legs.

Pl. 74

A fairly typical offering scene occurs on the lower register of the eastern wall in Room 3: offering-bearers are proceeding towards the princess. The first two make gestures of presentation of geese and a pilet duck (*Dafila acuta*) and those following carry platters or baskets full of victuals and lead young animals. One of the bearers is particularly laden: besides the platter with a large piece of meat on his shoulder, he is carrying on his arm a basket with yellow and green bands containing three ducks and a bundle of onions; in his left hand he holds by its wings a fourth duck, whose tail is being licked by a young calf following, held by a rope tied to a hind leg.

Pl. IX

On the eastern jamb of the passage between Rooms 3 and 4 the Princess Idut is shown standing, still bearing traces of the yellow ochre in which she was painted, and wearing the head-dress often worn by dancers (cf. Plate 53); she holds a lotus flower in each hand and sniffs the scent of the one in her left hand. In front of her are her titles written in two columns 'the daughter of the king, who is of his flesh and is revered after him alone, whom Hathor praises each day, revered beside Anubis on his mountain, Seshseshet, by his exalted name, Idut'.

Beyond the passage can be seen painted reliefs of the offering-bearers in Room 4. A notable feature here is the underside of the lintels, which are painted in pink to imitate granite, while to the left towards the top, the cavity for the door hinge still contains the remains of the wooden socket.

Pl. VIII

In Room 4, containing the false door stela, the bottom register of the southern extremity of the west wall shows three butchers quartering an ox that they have just slaughtered; while the first one from the left is sharpening his knife, the next one, who is about to cut off one of the rear legs, says to the third who is holding it firmly: 'pull towards you'. Beyond them two bearers are advancing, each with a hind quarter on his shoulder, the first carrying the beast's heart in his hand, and the second its ribs.

Above the register, a line of hieroglyphs explains that 'the inspectors of the *ka*'s servants and those attached to the *ka*'s service bring the best thighs for every feast and every day'; then, in a second register, three bearers ritualistically present two geese and a duck for the princess's table in front of which (above their heads) is a fine heap of provisions whose colours are still vivid and varied.

After the death of Firth, several most interesting mastabas were discovered near the temple and causeway of Unas. These will be described in Chapter VI, which deals with this royal funerary complex.

The sector situated to the north of the pyramid of Teti was the subject of further excavations by Zaki Y. Saad in 1942 and 1943, under Étienne Drioton, then Director-General. The northern extremities of the mastabas of Mereruka and Kagemni were completely cleared and this resulted in the discovery, in the north-western corner of Mereruka's tomb, of the funerary shaft of Meri-Teti, his son. To the north of these two large mastabas, a whole group of mastabas and lesser tombs, dating back to the VIth Dynasty, were also cleared. Some were of stone but the majority were of mud-bricks. Among the more interesting I need only mention the mastaba of Mereri described by Étienne Drioton.[65]

V, VI

THE MASTABA OF MERERUKA (MERY)

V The Room of Pillars, north wall (cf. p. 60). The painted limestone standing figure of Mereruka in its niche, on the frame of which are engraved his names and titles. Like stelae, the sides of the niche have a border of vertical, beribboned torus moulding. At the foot of the niche is an offerings table, approached by four steps. On the walls on each side, Mereruka is depicted walking away, preceded by his wife wearing a ribbon diadem and smelling a lotus flower, and followed by his mother; both women are shown below the level of his kilt.

Below the portraits, the black paint of the dado, and the two bands of yellow and red separating it from the bottom of the scenes in relief, are especially well preserved.

On the pillar at the right, Mereruka is seen wearing the sacerdotal panther-skin.

VI The Room of Pillars, north wall (cf. p. 61). Scenes showing the force-feeding of animals; note, in particular, the lower register with hyenas being fed.

V

VI

VII

VIII IX

## VII

THE MASTABA OF PTAH-HOTEP

Room 3, west wall, central section. Ptah-hotep, shown wearing the sacerdotal panther-skin, is seated before his table. On the right, lines of offering-bearers (in three registers) advance towards him (cf. p. 74).

## VIII, IX

THE MASTABA OF PRINCESS IDUT

VIII   Room 4, west wall, southern end (cf. p. 80). On the lower register three butchers are quartering an ox; one of these, who is preparing to sever a hind-leg, says to his colleague who is assisting, 'Pull towards you!' Beyond, two porters are seen, each carrying a leg on his shoulder, and one holding the heart and the other the ribs.

   On another register a generous pile of provisions, depicted in lively colours, is shown before the princess's table.

IX   Passage between Rooms 3 and 4 (cf. p. 80). The princess, shown standing on the east jamb, wears her hair in a style often associated with dancers; holding a lotus-flower in each hand, she sniffs the scent of one. Before her is engraved the inscription: 'the daughter of the king, who is of his flesh and is revered after him alone, whom Hathor praises each day, revered beside Anubis on his mountain, Seshseshet, by his exalted name, Idut'.

   Note the pink colouring below the lintels imitating granite and, on the left above, the cavity for the door-hinge with remains of the wooden socket.

# IV

## The Royal Necropolis of the Ist Dynasty

This royal necropolis was discovered, at the northern end of the site at Saqqara, through excavations carried out for the Service des Antiquités by Walter B. Emery, first with the collaboration of Zaki Y. Saad from 1936 to 1939,[66] then alone from 1946 to 1949.[67] In 1952, after an interruption of three years, the excavations were resumed by Emery, on behalf of the Egypt Exploration Society, and continued until 1956.[68]

The systematic exploration of the northern part of the desert plateau of Saqqara, from its northern edge overlooking the village of Abusir, to the house of the Antiquities Department Inspectorate, brought to light, in addition to several tombs of lesser importance, a dozen large panelled tombs in mud-brick. Inside these tombs, on clay jar-stoppers, were seal-impressions

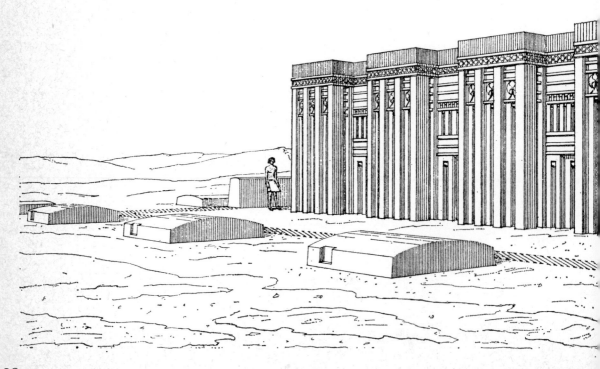

bearing *serekhs* (the name of each king written within a gateway – representing his palace – and surmounted by the divine falcon Horus). The Horus names of all the kings of the Ist Dynasty were represented, except those of Narmer, the first king, and Semerkhet, the penultimate one.

At first Emery thought that the tombs he was finding were those of high officials; their names – Hemaka, Ankhka, Nebitka – were impressed on jar-sealings found among others bearing the names of the royal Horus, and these names sometimes also appeared on various objects of funerary furniture. The discovery in 1938, however, of another vast panelled tomb (No. 3357), in which over seven hundred jar-stoppers bore the *serekh* of the Horus Aha to the exclusion of any other name, made Emery attribute the tomb to this king who, in fact, at Abydos, had only a much more modest funerary monument.[69] It was this fact that led Emery to suggest that the vast tomb No. 3035, which he had first believed to belong to Hemaka, chancellor of the Horus Udimu, was most probably the tomb of the king himself.[70]

Since then – and especially after the discovery in 1946 of several more large panelled tombs of the Ist Dynasty – the hypo-

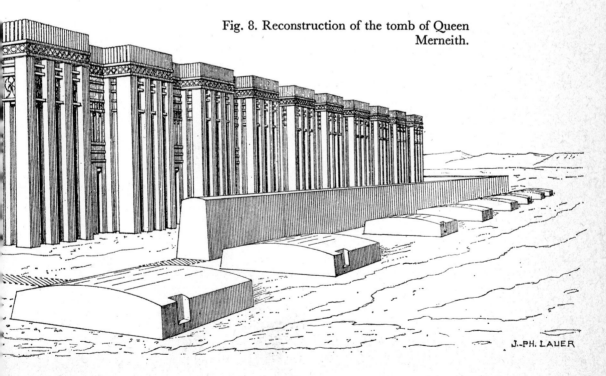

Fig. 8. Reconstruction of the tomb of Queen Merneith.

J.-PH. LAUER

thesis became stronger that here in fact were the royal tombs themselves, while those at Abydos were only cenotaphs. All the tombs here are much larger and more monumental than those of Abydos.[71] One of the former (No. 3504), which is probably the tomb of the Horus Djet (or Uadji, the famous Serpent King[72] whose magnificent limestone stela, discovered at Abydos, is in the Louvre), had on the low bench surrounding the vast panelled superstructure the remains of a row of clay bulls' heads fitted with large natural horns, probably taken from the numerous beasts sacrificed from the funeral of the king. Originally there must have been over three hundred heads representing a large herd of cattle assembled around the monument. Whether this was a symbolic offering or a magic protection, it is still difficult to determine, but if symbolic, these simulated bulls' heads would have served the same purpose as did the decorative reliefs of offerings of animals in the temples and mastabas of the Old Kingdom.

*Pl. 75*

This monument had, outside its perimeter and running parallel to it, a row of small subsidiary tombs with arched roofs, many of them still intact. (See Fig. 8, a reconstruction of the similar tomb of Queen Merneith. This type of façade does not, in fact, represent the front elevation of a palace as has often been said; it is only a repeated configuration of monumental palace doors, each of which is set between two towers or bastions. These dummy doors, measuring only 1·57 m. high by 0·52 m. wide are, evidently, at least half the size of real palace doors and must, therefore, be only smaller representations of them.) These subsidiary tombs were those of servants apparently sacrificed at the death of the principal personage to accompany him in the afterlife,[73] and this seems to confirm that he could only have been royal. Numerous jars, often bearing on their clay stoppers the seal-impression of the Horus Djet, the remains of a fine collection of stone vessels, and important fragments of rich furniture in wood and carved ivory were collected from this tomb.[74]

*Pl. 76*

Several of these large mud-brick tombs still had, on their panelled walls, traces of painting imitating wood, hangings or matting. Their contents afforded many surprises: a unique collection of objects and tools in copper was in the tomb attributed to the Horus Djer (No. 3471),[75] the successor of Aha; small discs of finely worked hardstone, remarkable carved flint knives, wooden sickles with a cutting edge formed by a row of small inset flint blades, intact hoe handles in carved wood, various types of arrows (including two with long sharp ivory tips), boxes

*Pl. 77*

and small cases with ivory inlay, etc. were in the so-called tomb of Hemaka,[76] which was probably, as noted above, that of the Horus Udimu, the successor of the 'Serpent King'.

Finally, the earliest known funerary temple, still containing the bases and feet of two wooden, nearly life-size statues, the most ancient that have survived, were discovered adjoining the northern face of a very large panelled tomb (No. 3505) within which were numerous seal-impressions of the Horus Ka'a.[77] This constitutes a major argument in favour of attributing the tomb to this king, the last of the Ist Dynasty.

The remarkable results obtained by Emery within this archaic necropolis, in addition (as we shall see in Chapter V) to the inscriptions engraved or written in ink on vessels of the same period discovered by J. E. Quibell and myself beneath the Step Pyramid, are the most important contributions made to the history of the Ist Dynasty since Flinders Petrie's excavations at Abydos around the beginning of this century.

# V

## The Funerary Complex of King Zoser or Djeser, the Horus Neterikhet

*Pls. 78, 94*

*Pl. 79*

In January 1924, before he had finished clearing the funerary complex of Teti's pyramid, C. M. Firth decided, in agreement with Pierre Lacau, then Director-General of Antiquities, to start the exploration of the Step Pyramid complex. He began by probing two small mounds situated to its north-east. Great was his surprise to find, at the foot of the southern face of each, the first courses, in beautifully dressed and finely jointed Tura limestone blocks, of a façade decorated with fluted engaged columns. These, like the Doric order, had sharp-edged flutings, and no bases. Could these be Greek columns? Soon the entrance passages of these two structures – the North and South Buildings – were cleared and on the walls were revealed important graffiti[78] in hieratic dating mainly from the XVIIIth and XIXth Dynasties. These graffiti indicate that those who came to the western desert to see the temple of Zoser found it 'as though heaven were within it, Re rising from it'. These scribes wish that 'all good and pure things fall [from heaven] to the *ka* of the justified Zoser' and they ask the gods 'presiding over the sacred Land', Osiris, Isis, etc., to grant them 'a good lifetime serving their *kas*'. Others hope to receive 'a good burial after a fine old age, in sight of the West of Memphis, like a great honoured one'. Finally, one of them who sees himself as 'a clever scribe without equal among any men of Memphis', strongly criticizes the graffiti of his predecessors, adding, 'my heart is sick when I see the work of their hands . . . It is like the work of a woman who has no mind; would that we had one who could have denounced them before ever they entered in to see the temple. I have seen a scandal, they are no scribes such as Thoth has enlightened.' There was therefore no doubt that these columns were very much older than the Greeks and must date back to the period of King Zoser of the IIIrd Dynasty (first half of the twenty-seventh century BC). This new discovery was very disconcerting: on the one hand, columns having various characteristics of the Doric order existing over 2,000 years before its birth in Greece; and, on the other, the use of small courses 20 to

25 cms in height, when the theory prevalent up till then was that stone architecture in Egypt had started with the use of large blocks.[79]

As the work of excavation progressed it produced surprise after surprise. First, there was the discovery of the startling life-size painted limestone statue of Zoser himself still in place in his *serdab* at the base of the north face of his Step Pyramid; Zoser is portrayed wearing a white cloak, which appears to be that worn by the king during the *heb-sed* (jubilee festival) ceremonies. He also wears the *nemes* head-dress curiously placed on a very large and bushy wig which falls down in front over his shoulders and also down his back. The eyes, from which the rock crystals have been torn out, and the badly mutilated nose add to the striking character of his fierce face and its very prominent cheekbones, thick lips and heavy jaw line. From Zoser's chin hangs a very long beard whose broken tip seems originally to have reached the right arm, shown folded across the chest, with closed fist. His left hand lies flat on his thigh. On the base of the statue the king's royal titles, in the name of Neterikhet, are carved in low relief. The statue is now in the Cairo Museum and a replica has been put in the *serdab* in its place.

*Pl. 80*

*Pls. 81, 82*

A few metres further away, the base of a ritual temple was discovered, also set against the north face, when all the pyramid temples previously known were set on the east side. In this temple, two interior courtyards had porticoed façades with engaged columns, also fluted, but here with bases.

*Pl. 83*

During the next campaign (1924–5), to the south-east of the pyramid, a spacious oblong courtyard was found. It was oriented north to south and, around it, were the remains of low staggered walls demarcating the entrances to small sanctuaries, each consisting of a single room containing a niche and having an open, dummy, hinged door carved in the stone.[80] Very numerous architectural elements, blocks, door jambs, sections of fluted columns, capitals with double fluted leaves, and cornice stones, etc. were scattered in the sand. At the south-western extremity of the courtyard, an eastward-running passage led to another smaller court; then, after a fine semi-circular perfectly made wall, there was a rectangular building with torus rolled corners, containing three fluted columns joined to the walls by supporting piers. These were still standing to a height of 1·40 m.

*Pl. 92*

*Pls. 84, 85*

In 1925–6, by extending the excavation southwards, the main entrance to this complex was reached. It was set in a bastion in the panelled enclosure wall of which only the first two or three

*Pl. X*

*Pl. 86*

*Pls. 87, 88*

*Pl. 89*

courses remained. Beyond the narrow passage from the entrance, two open dummy door-leaves, led to a small court. Then followed a second passage, shorter and slightly narrower, ending in another open dummy door but here having only one leaf. It opened into a magnificent gallery bordered by the remains of forty engaged columns, each joined to a low wall which abuts the long side walls. These columns, not fluted but reeded or fasciculated, were set on bases. They measured 1 m. in diameter at the base and about 0·70 m. under the abacus, had 17 or 19 stalks each and were markedly thicker than all those previously found in this complex.[81] This colonnade ended, towards the west, in a chamber placed at right-angles and containing eight columns which differ from the others in that they are in pairs, each pair being joined back to back. They must have supported a heavy stone roof made of beams placed on edge and rounded underneath to simulate thick logs; some of these roof beams were found nearby. From this chamber a final passage with an open dummy door placed in a panelled façade opened on to a vast courtyard that extended northward up to the pyramid. Another remarkable discovery was made here; this was of the famous pedestal of a statue of King Zoser, on which appears, in hieroglyphs, next to the name of the king, that of his famous minister Imhotep, preceded by all his titles: 'The chancellor of the King of Lower Egypt, the first after the King of Upper Egypt, administrator of the great palace, hereditary lord, the High Priest of Heliopolis, Imhotep the builder, the sculptor, the maker of stone vases . . .'[82]

By this fortunate find, we now see, emerging from the mists of legend, this extraordinary and venerated man who was deified much later, doubtless after the XXXth Dynasty, and in whom the Greeks, in their efforts at syncretization and because of his medical talents, had recognized their own god of medicine, Asclepios. Furthermore, under Ptolemy II, the Egyptian historian Manetho credited Imhotep with the invention of the art of building in dressed stone in regular courses. If the illustrious architect was not, strictly speaking, the first in Egypt to use dressed stone, prior to him it was used only in exceptional and sporadic cases in certain parts of structures built almost exclusively of mud-bricks, such as the cenotaph at Abydos of Khasekemwy, the last king of the IInd Dynasty. One can therefore imagine the profound impression made on the people of the time by the erection, for the tomb and the funerary cult of Zoser, of this prodigious complex, with its Step Pyramid completely encased in dressed stone, and its vast white panelled enclosure easily visible from the whole region of Memphis. Enormous prestige must have reflected not only on the king himself but also on his architect Imhotep. This can also explain why the latter made such a lasting impression on posterity and why he came, with the passing of the centuries, to be venerated as a god.

It was at this stage in the exploration of Zoser's vast funerary complex that its initiator, C.M.Firth, and P. Lacau, the Director-General of Antiquities, realized the necessity of entrusting the study of these buildings to an architect. They were so novel in character in Egypt and such a great number of architectural elements still lay scattered on the ground that they could, perhaps, be put back in place. It was then that I was called upon to assist Firth, and I arrived at Saqqara for an initial campaign of eight months' duration.

The first thing I undertook was to study the two buildings discovered by Firth at the north-east corner of the pyramid and which he had provisionally named as the tombs of the princesses Hetep-hernepti and Int-Ka-s whose names were found, together with that of Neterikhet (Zoser), on fragments of conical boundary stones or on stelae re-used, even during Zoser's time, in the construction of various thick walls nearby.

It very soon became apparent that the fluted columns in the principal façades of these buildings had a very noticeable batter: from 0·50 m. across the base to 0·28 m. under the fluted leaf capitals. Several examples of these capitals, of a type hitherto unknown, had been found during the excavations. If the batter had been the same all along the body of the columns, their height would have reached six to seven metres;[83] but a closer study, based on the measurement of all the separate column sections found, to see how they fitted and connected together and to find out which section belonged to which column, showed that this was not the case since the batter was much more pronounced at the bottom than towards the top. This gave a slight concavity to the general profile of the columns, meaning that the curve was the reverse of that of Greek or Roman columns, which are slightly convex or swollen. The columns thus shaped reached a height of 10·5–11 m. according to their position in the façade. They supported, but only in appearance, not in actuality, an arched band cornice which was actually held up by corbelling. Several cornice blocks, including the springing elements on each side of the band cornice,

Pl. 93

Pl. 92

Pl. 96

were found and their positions determined. These elements, together with the columns, enabled us to make drawings showing what these buildings, of a type otherwise unknown in Egypt, must have looked like in Zoser's day.[84] Furthermore, the study of these drawings showed that here, as with the Doric order, an attempt had been made to translate into stone the structure of buildings previously made of wood: the columns represent tree-trunks that formed the load-bearing elements, and the arched band represents the rafter that lay across horizontal beams whose ends are represented by the abacus of the capital placed between the two fluted leaves. These were probably stylized vegetable thongs used to strengthen the bonding of the column to the beam and to the rafter of the roof, the arched shape of the rafter being derived from that of predynastic shrines made of reeds, in which those used to make the roof were bent to give them extra strength. Finally, the peculiarity, slightly startling in these façades, of having a completely off-centre entrance between the two central columns and even flush against one of them, can also be explained by the translation into stone; entrance to the wooden prototype was through a hanging curtain or mat whose top fringe is stylized by the *kakeru* frieze which spans the whole façade and, since this curtain was necessarily loose, the entrance had to be set against a rigid part of the building, in this case one of the columns.

While I was occupied with the architectural research, Cecil Firth was carrying on with the clearing of the southern extremity of the complex, where fine remains of the beautiful panelled enclosure wall and bastions were uncovered, practically intact, for a length of nearly one hundred metres and to an average height of over four metres.

Towards the interior of the complex, and at the south-western corner of the great courtyard south of the pyramid, the enclosure wall formed a great projection that still carried the remains of a fine limestone single-panelled casing. At its foot lay several fragments of a frieze of cobras or uraei sculpted in the stone in high relief (see the reconstruction of the wall with replaced frieze in Plate 95).

From the terrace of the enclosure wall at the south-east of this projection, rose a curious superstructure of roughly hewn local limestone blocks. It was very elongated in its east-west axis and had a transversally arched top; some traces of a fine limestone casing were still apparent on its southern face. An ancient robbers' hole in this superstructure enabled the workmen to reach the steps of a blocked stairway; it was most likely a tomb whose attempted violation had been interrupted. Unfortunately, a second robbers' hole was soon found about fifty metres away towards the east and this revealed the existence of a great shaft through whose masonry filling the robbers had evidently succeeded, this time, in forcing an entrance.

Returning to the first robbers' hole, Firth started to unblock the faintly glimpsed stairway. He soon realized that it ran in a trench, between two magnificent, battered retaining walls, down to a tunnel through which the steps continued. At the entrance to this tunnel, still completely blocked with masonry, a passage ran off to the right and opened into a horizontal gallery about thirty metres long, containing a great quantity of large pottery jars and a wooden stretcher that had served to transport them, together with a set of long canopy poles still showing the remains of a gold overlay.

*Pl. 97*

In the tunnel itself, the staircases, once cleared, led to the great shaft disclosed by the second robbers' hole. The stairway, skirting a fine limestone-built chamber within the shaft, continued down a passage about one metre wide roofed by stone beams, placed side by side and rounded on the underside to simulate thick wooden logs.

In the front and to the left of the blocked entrance to the chamber, the steps continued downwards and eastwards into another tunnel. The clearing of this chamber was a time-consuming and delicate operation.[85] The ancient robbers had dug beneath its eastern and western walls, making it necessary to clear the great shaft above the chamber and then to strengthen the bases of its walls. Finally, after removing a thick layer of alabaster chippings mixed with the remains of a diorite pavement, we reached a granite floor in which was a narrow, semi-cylindrical hole that had been unblocked by the ancient robbers. It opened into another room, completely empty except for one of the granite blocks that must have been used as plugs to close the opening; this block of granite had grooves cut into its sides to take lifting ropes (see in Plate 98 the similar plug in the upper part of the burial chamber beneath the Step Pyramid).

We were able to determine, more or less, the mechanism for closing this burial chamber: it was operated from the room above, which was called for this reason the 'manœuvre chamber'.[86] One can still see a thick beam fitted into its east and west walls showing, on its upper surface, scorings that had evidently been caused by the friction of the ropes used to lower the various granite blocks into place. A second thick granite block with grooves for lifting ropes was found outside among the ruins of the temple of Unas, not far from the tomb.

The burial chamber, very similar to the one in the Step Pyramid itself, differs from it mainly in its shape, which is 1·60 m. square instead of being rectangular (1·60 × 2·40 m.). As it could not accommodate an extended body, nor even a life-size statue, it is very possible that it was destined to house the canopic jars containing the viscera of King Zoser, portions of his mummy (notably a foot) having been found in the burial chamber of his pyramid.[87]

Beyond the shaft, and after several bends in which some large alabaster vases had been deposited, the stairway reached a walled door. We made a hole in this door and Firth, who was rather corpulent, asked me to enter and describe what was inside. With feelings of great awe, I entered this subterranean gallery – 28 m. below ground level – which no one had set foot in since it was robbed during the First Intermediate period some 4,000 years ago; I made my way by the light of a candle, and found myself in an oblong room lined with finely dressed and carefully smoothed limestone. It led northwards into other rooms closed off with more blocks of dressed stone, some of which were decorated with large stars in low relief. Moving to the east through a passage whose walls had been prepared to receive small blue tiles like those under the Step Pyramid, I encountered in the half light one surprise after another: to the east of the first room and at right-angles to it was another room in which, on its western side, were six panels whose blue tiles had unfortunately been removed; many of them were lying on the

Pl. 99

floor. Each panel was crowned with an arch of *djed* pillars still retaining, in their tiered branches, a few small pieces of blue tiles in the shape of thin-veined leaves.

The threshold I had just crossed, which was through one of the panels, had a frame upon which, very finely carved, were the titles and the *serekhs* of the Horus Neterikhet (Zoser), exactly like the one removed from beneath the Step Pyramid by Lepsius in 1848 and sent to the Berlin Museum.

But it was in a third room, situated immediately to the south of the preceding one, that the major discoveries were made. Here were three dummy-door stelae, each bearing very concise and enigmatic texts around an extremely fine relief of King Zoser shown in one of the following symbolical attitudes: run-

ning a ritual race with his emblems of power, and founding two *Pl. XII*
religious sanctuaries, one in Upper and the other in Lower
Egypt. A roll, once fitted with blue tiles and simulating a rolled-
up mat, was in the upper part of each stela beneath the lintel,
itself topped by two dummy windows. These three dummy-door
stelae and the westward passage that followed, had frames *Pl. 100*
decorated with the royal titles similar to those on the door fitted
in one of the panels surmounted by *djed* pillars in the preceding
chamber.

The western passage was littered with fine limestone blocks
displaced by the robbers. After it had been cleared, we reached
a vestibule lying parallel to the chamber containing the dummy-
door stelae. In the eastern wall of this vestibule, false backs to
these stelae were carved, showing the dummy cross-members of *Pl. 101*
their panels. After the vestibule came a passage and a chamber
simply lined in fine limestone. These had to be cleared of all the
blocks that obstructed them, after which we reached, through
another passage with door frames similar to the preceding ones,
two other rooms decorated with blue tiles; some of these were
still in place, principally on the north wall of the second
chamber. In its western side was a hole made by robbers who
had come directly from the bottom of the main shaft, where they
had rediscovered and followed a narrow gallery used in the
digging and preparation of this group of rooms.

These last two blue-tiled rooms, with tiles on four sides, are
identical to those long known beneath the Step Pyramid. They
seem to represent the living quarters of the palace of the *ka*, the
first two rooms with the dummy-door stelae representing the
façade of the palace, and those with *djed*-pillar panels, the
façade of the adjacent store-rooms.

This important discovery led to another equally important
one. Cecil Firth, having re-examined the fragments of blue tiles
taken from the pyramid, noticed that some of them were of the
same shape and had the same ribbing as the small elements
ornamenting the *djed*-pillar branches in the South Tomb. He
therefore concluded that *djed* panels must also exist in the
underground chambers of the pyramid, and decided to clear
and examine these systematically.[88] His theory was proved to be
correct when two further blue-tiled rooms were found in 1928,
one containing three stelae of the king, similar to those in the
South Tomb, and the other, three *djed* panels *in situ* and prepared
parts of a fourth; these parts, whose placing had not been completed before the death of the king, had simply been deposited

97

Pl. 102

at the end of the room. Reconstructed by us, they make up the *djed*-pillar panel now displayed in the Cairo Museum.[89]

The same plan of underground rooms, containing similar blue-tiled panelled rooms, is therefore present both under the Step Pyramid and under the South Tomb. So the question arises: why are there, under the same monumental complex, two sets of nearly identical rooms, one, the most important in which some of Zoser's remains were found, situated under his pyramid, and the other, better finished, situated under the structure in the southern enclosure? In the latter the smaller size of the burial chamber could indicate that it was intended for the canopic jars containing the king's viscera. One can, however, wonder why they were buried two hundred metres away from the body.

It is convenient here to recall that the kings of the first two dynasties (called Thinite) each had two tombs built, one at Saqqara opposite their capital of Memphis, and the other, in most cases possibly only a cenotaph, in the ancestral necropolis of Om-el-Gaâb at Abydos; this, at least, is what the excavations and discoveries made by W. B. Emery at Saqqara seem to indicate. In my opinion it is probable that King Zoser, who did not come from an Upper Egyptian family but belonged to a new dynasty issuing from Memphis, did not feel the urge to build a cenotaph so far south. Nevertheless he felt that he should represent this cenotaph symbolically at the southern extremity of the vast funerary complex, to the building of which his inspired minister-architect Imhotep was devoting all his talents.[90]

Various complementary explorations in the Zoser complex were undertaken by Firth. He found in the northern area near a vast rock-cut altar, simulated store-rooms above subterranean galleries containing great quantities of provisions of wheat, barley, sycamore figs and grapes[91] and, to the west, three galleries about four hundred metres long from which branched, at right-angles, a considerable number of oblong chambers. A vast quantity of stone and pottery vessels was found as well as various animal bones and a skeleton in a contracted position;[92] unfortunately, the insecure state of the roofs of these galleries prevented the systematic clearing which alone would have made possible a proper interpretation of their use.

In addition, Firth authorized me, while he was away from the site working in Nubia, to undertake various clearances necessary to further our researches. Thus the east and west faces of the pyramid itself were cleared and the appearance of its successive casings enabled me to determine the construction stages of the monument. Furthermore, we probed the perimeter of the enclosure wall in order to locate the bastions with double-leaf dummy doors which this wall must have contained. There were fourteen such bastions placed irregularly on the eastern side of the enclosure, but quite regularly in the case of those on the other three sides.[93] Finally, the clearing of the great courtyard south of the pyramid up to its base, the last important area in the Zoser complex, was carried out under my direction in 1939, several years after Firth's death. We found, at the foot of the pyramid, small granite statues of the Old Kingdom and a quite remarkable head of a woman in stuccoed and painted wood, wearing large disc ear-rings. Its very long and straight neck is reminiscent of the Old Kingdom heads known as 'reserve heads', but although it was discovered in the sand at the foot of the Step Pyramid, it cannot be older than the end of the XVIIIth Dynasty and is possibly much more recent.[94]

*Pl. 112*

Concurrently with my work on the theoretical reconstruction of the Zoser monuments, I made many attempts to fit the column sections to the fasciculated columns of the entrance hall where, at the time of Firth's death, we had already succeeded in replacing over three hundred elements in their original positions.[95] In 1933 I succeeded in completing the reconstruction of the eight coupled columns in the chamber at the western end of the entrance hall.[96]

*Pls. 90, 91*
*Pls. 86, 87*

*Pl. 88*

In addition, during the same campaign of 1932–3, and in collaboration with J. E. Quibell who had returned to Saqqara to publish Firth's notes on his excavations in the Zoser complex, I resumed the exploration (which Firth's death prevented him from undertaking) of the deepest underground galleries beneath the Step Pyramid. We found a new gallery running east to west. It contained some traces of wooden panelling and, towards its western end, two fine alabaster sarcophagi: the first was placed against the southern wall and was empty, the second was placed transversally against the western end and still contained the bones of an eight-year-old child within the remains of a coffin whose sides were made of six thin superimposed layers of wood with the grain alternating as in modern plywood. The outer layer was vertically grooved like ribbed velvet or corduroy and had been originally covered with chased gold-leaf fitting into grooves and held in place with small gold nails. The gold-leaf had been stripped by the robbers and only some small fragments of it and a few nails remained.[97] Protruding from the south face of the gallery, against the sarcophagus, were fragments of stone vessels. As we extracted them, more were revealed and it soon became apparent that they must have come from an adjoining gallery; but it would have been dangerous to try to reach it from here because of the very bad state of the crumbling rock of the partition and the presence of the sarcophagus whose position left no room to carry out the necessary consolidation. We therefore chose a point, seventeen metres back, where the ancient robbers had started an attempt to tunnel towards the south, and began excavating. After more than a day of hard work, we were most surprised to come upon an extraordinary heap of partly crushed stone vessels that completely filled, from the floor to the ceiling (1·55 m.), the gallery we were seeking.

*Pl. 103*

The clearing of this thirty-metre long gallery and of a similar one also filled with vessels that joined it before passing underneath, was going to take several months.[98] It required the removal of 36–40,000 vases, bowls and stone dishes, mostly crushed by the partial subsidence of the ceilings of the galleries. These had never been reached by the ancient robbers and therefore the collection of crushed vessels must, in principle, be complete, and hence it was important to avoid mixing the fragments as far as possible in order to facilitate their reconstruction.

After having tried, systematically and separately, to wrap up in a single piece of paper, the pieces of a single object, we soon found that the handling of these packages was difficult, not to say precarious. We therefore decided to use easily carried wooden boxes into which several packages could be grouped as they were extracted. The making of these boxes was immediately started, and eventually some six thousand were made. Each was numbered and marked with the removal date of the vessels they contained, each box containing an average of six packages. To the fragments of 36,000 vessels thus extracted must be added all the broken vessels removed before we started to use boxes, and also the few hundred specimens we found complete. It is therefore no exaggeration to assert that about 40,000 vessels of all shapes, bowls, cups, dishes with and without feet, had been buried in these galleries. The majority were made of Egyptian alabaster (calcium carbonate), whose beautiful veining was fully exploited by the makers of the vessels, as can be seen in a selection of these vases lit from inside. The other materials used were, in order of frequency: bluish or greenish

*Pl. 106*

30 Entrance, east panel: Mereruka is shown seated before a picture on an easel. He holds his paint-brush in one hand and, in the other, a shell used as a palette; he is painting the (three) seasons, each represented by a divinity. His son Khenenu, on a much smaller scale, approaches with his ink palette in his hand.

31 Room 1, north wall: hunting in papyrus marshes (see pp. 56–7).

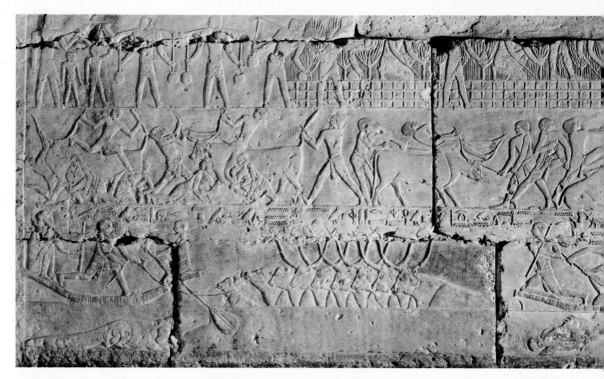

32–36  THE MASTABA OF MERERUKA

32  Room 1, south wall, near the south-east corner (reading from the bottom): cattle crossing a swamp; men capturing sacrificial oxen; watering gardens (see pp. 57–8).

33  Room 2, west wall: hunting in the desert (see pp. 58–9).

34  Room 2, east wall (reading from the top):

groups of men pulling a funerary shrine; goldsmiths at work; making necklaces (see pp. 59–60).

35  Room 3, west wall: a scene from a law court (see p. 60).

36  Room 4, west wall: an intimate musical scene. Mery squats on a large canopied bed with lions'-paw feet, while his wife sits facing him playing the harp; to the left and right, male and female dancers move in line.

34

35

36

37  The Mastaba of Mereruka, Room of Pillars. North wall, above the doorway to the passage leading north: adolescent games (see pp. 60–1).

38–40 THE MASTABA OF MERERUKA, ROOM OF PILLARS

38 West wall: large sailing boats with crane-masts (see p. 62).

39 South wall, to the east of the entrance passage:

an otter has caught a mullet, while a crocodile and other fish can be seen in the water below (see p. 62).

40 East wall, north end: Mery, seated at the left with his wife, playing a game of *zenet* with his smaller partner opposite; the rest of this relief shows bearers bringing offerings (see p. 62).

41 Room of Pillars,
north wall: Mery, flanked
by his two sons, walking
together with hands
joined in a curious manner;
all three are wearing the
long skirt with triangular
apron almost reaching the
ankles.

42 Room 6, in the part of
the mastaba reserved for
his wife, the Princess
Har-watet-khet: at the left,
the false door resembling
the entrance to a palace
and, on the north wall, the
princess seated at the
traditional table (see pp.
62–3).

*Opposite*
43–45 THE MASTABA OF KAGEMNI

43 Room 2, east wall: a group of five
short-haired dancers performing a ballet,
apparently defying the laws of gravity (see p.
63 and compare pl. 53).

44 Room 2, north wall, to the left of the
passage: fishing with a net and a multi-
hooked line from a papyrus boat; on the left
is the stern of Kagemni's boat (see pp. 63, 68).

45 Room 2, north wall, near the west end:
a cow being milked and another suckling a
calf, and, in the lower register, cattle crossing
a stretch of water (see p. 68).

46–49 THE MASTABA OF
KAGEMNI

46 Room 2, north wall: a
breeder, seated on a low reed
chair, holds in front of his
face a suckling pig which is to
be weaned; in order to begin
its meal, drops of milk have
been placed on the man's
tongue which the animal then
licks. Above, a greyhound is
seen feeding.

47 Room 3, north wall:
Kagemni, whose name and
titles (including those of
vizier and minister of justice)
are inscribed above his arm,
is seated on his carrying
chair (see p. 68).

48 Room 3, west wall, southern half: the lower register shows a bird-hunting scene, using a net; above this is an aviary with ducks and geese being fed; the damaged top register shows geese being forcibly fed with specially prepared pellets of food set set out on trays (see pp. 68–9).

49 Room 3, west wall, northern end: another scene of geese being forcibly fed (see p. 69) and, in the upper register, hyenas being forcibly fed (cf. the similar scene shown in colour plate VI).

50 Room 1, east side of the north
doorway: two stages in a circumcision
operation and, above, a patient
apparently having his leg incised or
massaged.

51 Room 1, west side of the north
doorway: two patients undergoing
treatment, one (on the right) to his
big toe, the other to the thumb of his
right hand.

52 Room 3, north wall of the passage leading west: in the lower panel an oryx and a dorcas gazelle are each led by two men; above, six men are engaged in bringing down a magnificent ox, supervised by their overseer at the right (see p. 70).

53, 54 THE MASTABA OF ANKH-MA-HOR
53 Room 2, south wall, to the east of the door: female dancers performing an acrobatic dance, similar to the scene in pl. 43.

54 Room 2, south wall, to the west of the door: below, a procession of dignitaries followed by male and female mourners and, above, more dignitaries in procession (see pp. 70–1).

55, 56
THE MASTABA OF PTAH-HOTEP
AND AKHET-HOTEP

55 Room 1, west wall: Akhet-hotep, shown on a very large scale standing on the right, and harvest scenes (see p. 71).

56 Room 3, dedicated to Ptah-hotep, central area of east wall: delivery of cattle and fowls before a walking figure of Ptah-hotep (the staff and arm only are shown) preceded by his son Akhti-hotep shown as a child (see p. 71).

57, 58 THE MASTABA OF PTAH-HOTEP AND AKHET-HOTEP

57 Room 3, upper part of east wall (reading from the bottom): scenes of cord twisting, a desert hunt occupying two registers, the grape harvest, adolescent games, and two scenes at the top showing cattle crossing a ford and the gathering of papyrus (see pp. 72–3).

58 A continuation of the scenes in pl. 57 (reading from the bottom): a man offering a goose to Ptah-hotep and men, manoeuvring small reed boats laden with various provisions, exchanging blows with their poles; netting wild ducks and geese; workmen finishing off papyrus boats (see pp. 73–4).

59  Mastaba of Ptah-hotep and Akhet-hotep, Room 3, north end of east wall: Ptah-hotep, depicted on a large scale, is shown walking, preceded by his son (also called Ptah-hotep). In front of them are the registers illustrated in pls 57 and 58 (see p. 74).

61–63 THE MONASTERY OF ST JEREMIAH

61 Niche from a monk's cell, with a beautiful fresco showing the Virgin suckling the Child between two angels. Coptic Museum, Cairo.

62 Watercolour copy, by Mrs J. E. Quibell, of a fresco representing the founding saint.

63 The pulpit, seen *in situ*, set against the wall of the courtyard to the south of the refectory, and directly to the east of the doorway linking them (see p. 75). Now Coptic Museum, Cairo.

*Opposite*
60 The pyramid of Unas: the antechamber showing the walls covered with the famous Vth Dynasty hieroglyphic 'Pyramid Texts' (see pp. 75, 143, 156).

64–66 Three of the magnificent capitals (sixth century AD) from the main building of the Monastery of St Jeremiah (see p. 75).

*Opposite*
67–69 THE MASTABA OF KA-IRER

67 Marsh scene, with a crocodile laying its eggs.

68 Scene showing the weighing of ingots using a very curious balance in the form of a woman with outstretched arms (see p. 77).

69 Relief showing flute-players in the upper two registers and a game of *zenet* in the lower one (cf. pl. 40).

70   Room 1, north wall, to the right of the passage: in front of the princess's large boat, fishermen in a reed-boat are using a dip-net and multi-hooked line (see pp. 78–9).

71   Passage between Rooms 1 and 2, west jamb: the statue of the princess, to which a priest offers incense, being dragged on a sledge by three men (cf. pl. 23).

72   Room 2, west wall: the princess in her boat, watching a hippopotamus hunt (see p. 79).

73   Detail showing the crocodile and the hippopotamus giving birth, from the scene in pl. 72.

74   Room 3, east wall, lower register: offering-bearers proceeding towards the princess (see p. 80).

72

73

74

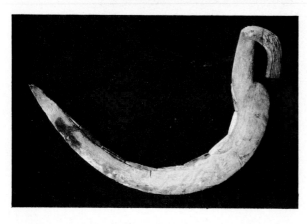

75–77 THE ROYAL NECROPOLIS OF THE
1ST DYNASTY

75 Mud-brick panelled tomb attributed to
the Horus Djet, or Uadji: view of some of the
300 bulls' heads modelled in clay and fitted
with natural horns (see p. 88).

76 One of the panelled tombs with traces of
painted decoration representing matting or
hangings (see p. 88).

77 Wooden sickle with a cutting edge of
inset flints, found in the tomb said to be that
of Hemaka (see pp. 88–9).

78 Remains of the façade
of the North Building,
with fluted engaged
columns in the style of the
Doric order.

79    Example of hieratic
graffiti in the entrance
corridor of the South
Building; such graffiti,
found in both the North
and the South Buildings,
mostly date from the
XVIIIth and XIXth
Dynasties (see p. 90).

80  Statue of King Zoser, life size, in painted limestone found in the *serdab* at the base of
Step Pyramid (see p. 91). Cairo Museum.

81 The statue of Zoser (cf. pl. 80), as discovered in the *serdab*.

82 Front view of the *serdab*, with its open dummy doors.

83  Scale model of one of the porticos with fluted engaged columns, forming part of the façade of Zoser's funerary temple fronting onto the two main inner courtyards (see p. 91).

84, 85  Pavilion in the courtyard with torus rolled corners, seen (opposite) in the state in which it was discovered and (above) after re-erection of the three columns (see p. 91).

86 The colonnaded entrance hall of Zoser's funerary complex, as discovered in 1926 (see p. 92). Note, at the exit from the colonnade into the courtyard, the half-open door-leaf on the left imitated in stone and framed on either side by the fine remains of a panelled wall.

87 The four groups of paired columns at the west end of the entrance hall, as excavated in 1926.

88 The groups of paired
columns (cf. pl. 87) after
restoration and
reconstruction.

89　The base of a
lost statue of Zoser;
the central part of the
relief gives the King's
names and *serekh*,
and on the left,
separated by a *djed*
pillar, are the names
and titles of the
minister-architect
Imhotep (see p. 92).

90, 91  Two views of the model reconstruction, by the author, of the funerary complex of King Zoser.

92 The capital of a fluted column in one of the chapels of the *heb-sed* courtyard (see p. 94). The deep round hole beneath the abacus (on which a rafter would lie) no doubt held a pole carrying a symbol representing the deity of the chapel.

93 Reconstruction drawing by the author, showing the South Building in Zoser's funerary complex; the reconstruction was based on the various scattered elements – columns, cornice and *kakeru* frieze – found during the excavations (see p. 94).

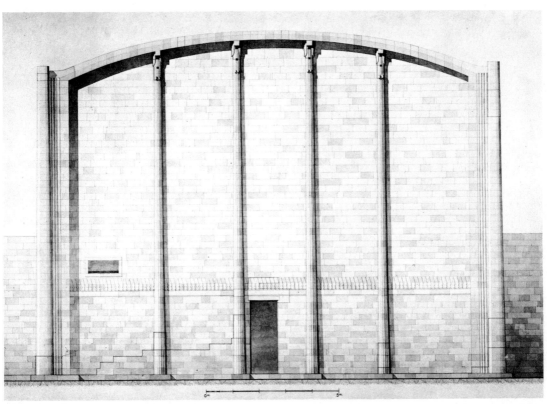

94–96 THE FUNERARY COMPLEX OF KING ZOSER

94 The South Building after restoration and partial reconstruction.

95 The Wall of Uraei (of which only the bottom third was found in place) after restoration and reconstruction using original stones; it forms the western wall of the sanctuary façade of Zoser's South Tomb (see p. 94).

96 Remains of the southern enclosure of the complex; the highest surviving part of the wall measures 4.60 m. (see p. 94).

schists from the Wadi Hammamat, red breschia from Assiut, and numerous varieties of diorite, porphyritic rock, dolorite, Aswan granite, dolomite, marble, serpentine, aragonite, quartz, and rock crystal.[99] Some of these vessels are remarkable not only for the purity of their form and the perfection of their workmanship, especially when in such hard materials, but also for the originality of their design, such as the curious alabaster vase on which a raised allegoric decoration expresses the hope that the king would celebrate one million *sed* festivals (jubilees), meaning: may he reign eternally. Other vases translate into stone forms details peculiar to pottery, to basket-work and even to metal, simple fantasies on the part of the craftsmen or re-presentations in stone – which was considered indestructible – of certain useful objects made of fragile or perishable materials, for use in the afterlife. Did this idea (also revealed in stone models of offerings of food discovered in many tombs of the Old Kingdom) not have many applications on a vaster scale when Imhotep petrified the shapes of archaic symbolic buildings made of light materials, in front of which the king had to celebrate his *heb-sed* in the afterlife?

*Pl. 105*

*Pl. 104*

*Pls. 107, 108*
*Pl. 109*

The numerous inscriptions found on these stone vessels were of two types: those carved giving the titles or the name of the owner, king or noble, and sometimes the royal monument to which the vessels were destined (162 examples);[100] and the others, numbering more than a thousand, which bore several hundred different texts. They were usually written in black or, more rarely, red ink. They give the name of the donor or the maker, the occasion for the gift, which was often the *sed* festival, workshop marks and sometimes measurements.[101] These examples of cursive writing that mostly date from the Ist or IInd Dynasties are, together with the few others previously collected at Abydos, the most ancient that we possess. They prove that hieroglyphic writing was already highly developed, and constitute valuable palaeographic documents for the study of the formation of hieratic writing that was to appear during the IVth Dynasty.

The engraved inscriptions are also historically important since they give the names of nearly all the kings of the Ist and IInd Dynasties and sometimes even short lists of the succession of many of them; but the name of Neterikhet (Zoser) is never mentioned though it was he who had caused these galleries to be excavated. Only one large clay seal was found bearing, on one side, the king's name in his *serekh* and, on the other, the imprint of a cloth that must have been used to wrap up a collection of dishes. It seems therefore that Zoser did not want to appropriate for himself these vessels manufactured long before his reign, and this might have been an act of piety on his part: he had buried, under his pyramid which was considered inviolable, vessels that had been collected from ransacked tombs of his predecessors and, in so doing, ensured their returning to their rightful owners for their use in the afterlife.

Several other galleries were discovered parallel to the previous ones and on the same level, but they only contained some pottery, a few scattered vases of stone and metal and various objects and tools that had been left behind when, during Zoser's time, it was decided to refill the galleries with the debris resulting from their excavation.

My work of reconstruction, which I had interrupted in order to concentrate on these explorations beneath the Step Pyramid, could only be resumed during the campaigns of 1936–7, principally on the two symbolic buildings that we named the 'Houses of the North and of the South'. The latter was partially restored and, in the courtyard of the North Building, small papyrus columns, emblems of the Kingdom of the North, were restored to their original form.[102] During the two subsequent campaigns (1938 and 1939) we undertook the reconstruction of a part of the beautiful panelled wall that formed the façade of the South Tomb's sanctuary. This wall was named the 'wall of Cobras or Uraei' because of the elements of a frieze of uraei that we had replaced upon its crest.[103]

*Pls. 93, 94*

*Pl. XI*

*Pl. 95*

The restoration, projected in 1939, of the enclosure wall and its bastions that are part of the main entrance, had been started with new stones in my absence during the Second World War. Fortunately, well-justified protests put a stop to this practice; but I was only able to resume the reconstruction work I had recommended, on my return from France in 1946.[104] In this manner we restored and incorporated, not only the elements of the parapet and the cat-walk, but also numerous blocks with small square recesses that probably copied the ends of the strengthening wooden joists that used to be embedded in the higher courses of large brick walls.

*Pl. X*

This enclosure wall had a batter that made it possible to determine its height with mathematical precision: it was exactly 20 cubits (about 10·50 m.). Finally, at the rear of the entrance where the door leaves are represented in stone, we replaced the two enormous stone dummy hinges. This reconstruction of the façade, often interrupted by lack of funds, was completed only in 1956.[105] After this, international events again put a stop to the work that still remained to be done on the cat-walk and on the platform above the entrance. It could only be resumed and completed after my return in 1959, thanks to the goodwill and understanding of Dr Saroite Okacha, at that time Minister of Culture in Egypt.

At the same time, from 1960, I undertook new restorations and reconstructions in the main group of monuments of the *heb-sed*. In the main courtyard reserved, inside the funerary enclosure of Zoser, for this jubilee festival for his *ka* in the hereafter, the only objects preserved more or less partially in place were the low staggered walls and the bases of chapels and pavilions of a symbolic character that copy, in stone, buildings in wood or brick, themselves imitating predynastic reed sanctuaries, or made of wattling or puddled clay. During the excavations we had gathered together numerous stones belonging to these constructions, mainly sections and capitals of fluted columns, torus mouldings, door jambs, the crowning elements of walls and roofs, etc. By studying these diverse elements, I had been able to publish, since 1928, exact reconstruction drawings of these buildings, and it appeared to be most interesting and desirable to attempt the reconstruction of each of the predynastic types represented by the fragments, and easily recognizable thanks to the extraordinary petrification realized by Imhotep, 4,700 years ago.

We started with an arched-roof chapel and its slender fluted columns. Its principal façade was reconstructed in 1963 and its rear in 1965. In this stone translation, the wooden elements are positively represented as such by the columns with their fluted shafts that were previously made of wood, by the abaci of their capitals manifestly representing the ends of the beams supported by the columns, and by the cornice representing a strong arched rafter.[106]

*Pl. XIII*

The pavilion with torus corners and flat roof of the second type was started in the winter of 1963–4. Its principal façade was completed in the spring of 1968 and its sides and rear the following year.

*Pl. XIV*

The remarkable curved wall that bounds the terrace situated to the west of the back of the last-mentioned pavilion, was reconstructed to its original height at the end of 1967.[107]

*Pl. III*

Finally, the reconstruction of a third type of chapel, situated to the east of the *heb-sed* courtyard and having an arched roof but no columns, was started at the beginning of 1969, with the collaboration of my assistant, the Egyptian architect Salah el-Naggar.[108] This reconstruction was completed in the spring of 1973.[109]

*Pl. 110*

We are now proceeding with the reconstruction and re-erection of the main façade of a second chapel of the first type. It has an arched top and fluted columns also, but differs markedly from the one already rebuilt as it includes a set of stairs leading to a large niche that must have contained a statue.

# VI

## The IIIrd Dynasty Funerary Complex of the Horus Sekhemkhet

Discovered in 1950 by the Egyptian Egyptologist Zakaria Goneim, who died tragically in 1959, this monumental complex must originally have comprised a step pyramid and a bastioned and panelled enclosure wall, both very similar to those of Zoser.[110] Nothing remains of the core of the pyramid except part of the foundations, mostly of the sides and corners. Its panelled enclosure wall is completely destroyed but there still exists, to the north of the pyramid, a good part of a first but less extensive enclosure wall that had been abandoned by the builders after it had reached a height of six cubits (3·10 m.). The whole of this funerary complex, dating from the IIIrd Dynasty (end of the twenty-seventh century BC) and very probably built by Zoser's successor, had obviously not been completed. Nevertheless, the sloping trench-like entrance to the pyramid had been carefully blocked. After it had been cleared, a small deposit of jewellery was found[111] which included a gold scallop-shaped box, and, close by, numerous vases in hardstone and alabaster, intermixed with typical IIIrd Dynasty pottery and some clay stoppers. These bore seal-impressions in the name of Horus Sekhemkhet, a king still unknown except in the Wadi Maghara in Sinai where his name, incorrectly read on his stelae erected there, had been mistaken for that of Horus Semerkhet of the Ist Dynasty.[112]

Some forty metres inside the pyramid, the sloping descent reached a subterranean chamber, the entrance of which was still blocked. Inside was a curious alabaster sarcophagus, closed at one end by a vertically sliding panel, in which two holes had been bored to take lifting ropes.[113] When Zakaria Goneim succeeded in opening it, it was found to be empty. Had it contained the royal mummy? This was the question posed by the disappointing discovery. To find the answer, additional explorations in this complex had to be made; it was necessary to find the second tomb that Sekhemkhet must probably have built in the southern part of his complex – as did his predecessor Zoser and likewise his successors who also had a small satellite

*Fig. 9*

*Pl. 114*

*Pl. 113*

*Pl. 115*

*Pl. 116*

pyramid erected, first to the south of the royal pyramid, then, starting with the second king of the Vth Dynasty, at its south-eastern corner. Having died before his pyramid could be completed, had Sekhemkhet perhaps been buried in the southern tomb whose superstructure could be completed much more rapidly? It was in order to check these possibilities that I obtained, in 1963, permission to resume the excavation of this complex.

Although explorations in its southern part did not succeed in finding traces of a shaft or a tunnel entrance in the ruins of the great platform built at the edge of the complex on that side, one of our exploratory trenches did, however, reveal foundations at the same distance from the southern face of the pyramid as the remains of the previously mentioned panelled enclosure were from its northern face. It became apparent, therefore, that the initial complex was only 500 cubits (about 260 m.) long and that it had been enlarged to 1,040 cubits to equal Zoser's complex (see Fig. 9). But the enlargement was much more pronounced towards the northern than towards the southern side, where the presence of a wadi limited the possibilities of further expansion.[114]

This discovery was important because it showed that, in all probability, if a southern tomb had been planned in the funerary complex, it must have been at the time of the initial plan, and therefore much nearer to the pyramid and within the perimeter of the first enclosure, and that was where the search for it had to be made.

Our attention was thus drawn to a vast pocket of sand about twenty metres from the pyramid. We started clearing it and, during several campaigns (1965 to 1967) and with very rudimentary equipment, we removed a considerable amount of sand and debris, finally to reach the predicted remains of a southern tomb. These consisted of part of the foundations and a completely destroyed mastaba whose superstructure must have risen above the general level of the platform surrounding the pyramid. Its plan was rectangular, proportioned 1 : 2 and measuring 16 × 32 m., the longer side being oriented west to east. We next located near the west end of the building a vast shaft three metres square. Its upper part was built of random rubble and after a few metres was cut in the natural rock, the shaft having been filled up. After clearing the shaft and reaching the bottom, we found, opposite the burial chamber, the opening of a very steep sap coming from the west. It became apparent

*Pl. 117*

that ancient robbers had reached the bottom of the shaft by this route, forced their way through the filling and penetrated the burial chamber.[115] This chamber was a simple, straight gallery roughly hewn in the rock and measuring 2·10 m. wide, 2·30 m. high and 17·50 m. long. The gallery widened slightly three or four metres before its end, no doubt to form the actual burial chamber. But this one was empty; however, lying across the gallery about five metres from the shaft, was a flattened wooden sarcophagus of a type common during the earliest dynasties. After letting it dry, we investigated its contents and were greatly surprised to find the dislocated skeleton of a two-year-old boy with a completely shattered skull. The child was certainly not the king, who would have rated a more luxurious coffin made of alabaster or hardstone. It could only be a young prince who died a short time after his father's death, perhaps during a distant campaign, and this might explain why the king's body was not buried beneath his pyramid and why the building of his funerary monument had suddenly been cut short.[116]

*Pl. 118*

The access passage to the pyramid in which a few offerings had been placed, had, nevertheless, been carefully blocked. As to the unfinished south tomb, the part of it that was available had been used to bury this royal child of the IIIrd Dynasty. This is what the remains of some funerary furniture seem to

Fig. 9. Plan of the funerary complex of the Horus Sekhemkhet, showing the principal pyramid, the South Tomb (*a*) and exploratory shafts (*s*). Distances are shown in cubits (see text). After Lauer.

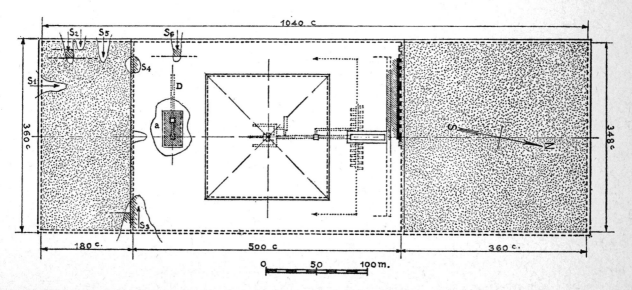

indicate: the stone vases typical of the period, the fragments of gold-leaf imprinted with the design of matting on the wood it had covered, a very frequent pattern during the earliest dynasties, and the small cornelian incrustations, not to mention the short sarcophagus also characteristic of this period – all of which are proof that this was not a possible later usurpation.

The most recent researches undertaken here, authorized by Dr Gamal Mokhtar, President of the General Organization for the Antiquities of Egypt, have made it possible to reach two important conclusions: first, the South Tomb was violated, shortly after the burial of the royal child, by somebody with an intimate knowledge of the plan of the descent arrangements; further, this descending passage also provided access – but from the opposite side – to an underground entrance to the west which it will be necessary to clear. It must correspond with the galleries from which had been extracted the vast quantity of marl needed for the building of the high and extensive platform surrounding the tomb. The exploration of these galleries could be the source of still more surprises.

# VII

## The Vth Dynasty Funerary Complexes of Kings Userkaf and Unas

It was Cecil M. Firth who, in 1928, discovered the principal remains of the funerary temple of Userkaf[117] situated, contrary to custom, to the south of an unidentified pyramid which some scholars had attributed to Isesy, the predecessor of Unas. Of this temple, nothing remains in place but some portions of a beautiful basalt pavement on which it is possible to determine the positions of the granite pillars and of the walls, in which granite sills indicate the positions of the doors. In addition, some remarkable scattered fragments of very high-quality reliefs bore several cartouches of Userkaf, and this made it possible to attribute positively to that king the temple and the adjacent principal pyramid.

*Pl. 119*

Two other much smaller pyramids were cleared, one to the west and the other to the south of the temple. The first and smaller one contained nothing at the end of its descending passage (unblocked just sufficiently to allow a man to pass), except a small empty room with a flat ceiling; it would have been impossible to remove a sarcophagus from there. This must surely be a satellite pyramid such as was afterwards found near the south-eastern corner of the royal pyramids in all the funerary complexes of the Vth and VIth Dynasties. The second small pyramid, that had some traces of a funerary temple adjoining its eastern face, belonged to a queen who must have been Userkaf's wife. It had later served as a quarry and revealed, in its centre, the burial chamber whose vaulted ceiling, composed of huge inverted V-shaped stone blocks, had been partly smashed open and largely destroyed.

A very fine discovery was made in the porticoed courtyard of the royal pyramid's temple while clearing the cavities in which the granite pillars had stood: in one of them was found a magnificent colossal head of Userkaf, in beautifully finished pink granite; this is now in the Cairo Museum. Although the rest of the body was missing, the head is, with the exception of the Sphinx at Giza, the only example of a colossal statue to have survived from the Old Kingdom.

*Pl. 120*

Userkaf's temple had been further damaged by the construction of some important Saite (sixth century BC) mastabas whose enormous shafts, in some cases covering over 100 square metres, were the cause of the disappearance here of all trace of the temple's ground plan. One of these shafts measuring over ten metres a side contained, at a depth of twenty metres, the twin tombs of Neferib-re-sa-neith and Wahib-re-men, the latter's tomb being intact[118] and still containing some small items of gold jewellery and amulets, mostly in cornelian, lapis lazuli or haematite, and including a large heart scarab of dark-green jasper.[119] All these finds are now displayed in the Cairo Museum.

*Pl. 121*

Firth, who had published a hasty and incomplete drawing of the temple's ground plan, was unable to finish the exploration, and this led Zaki Saad to carry out, in 1941–2, some supplementary work on this temple site. But this had to be focused on the emptying of another great shaft, eight metres square, belonging to Hor, a noble of the Saite period.[120] After this had been done the site was abandoned.

It was only after the Second World War, from 1949 to 1953, that we were able, although hampered by extremely meagre means and frequent stoppages resulting from lack of funds, to resume work on reconstituting this temple's ground plan, one which deserved special attention due to its unusual placing to the south of the pyramid.[121] I was able to ascertain that, although the greater part of the temple had been built to the south probably owing to lack of space on the east, a small sanctuary for offerings had, nevertheless, been built against the eastern face of the pyramid. This sanctuary contained a central chamber paved in basalt and two service rooms placed on each side. The central chamber, whose entrance was on its axis, had two granite pillars to carry the roof; it must have sheltered a stela, the only remains of which were some quartzite fragments found lying there.

The entrance to the temple was finally located in its eastern wall near its south-eastern corner and, from there, I was able to find the traces of the vestibules that gave access to the porticoed courtyard. It was also at that time, while searching for stone to use in the reconstruction of Zoser's enclosure wall, that I discovered among a group of tombs of the Old Kingdom the *serdab* of Isheti,[122] a chancellor who held office during the VIth Dynasty, still containing a number of interesting wooden statues.

*Pls. 122–4*

*The Funerary Complex of Unas*

More than half a century earlier, at the pyramid of Unas, Maspero had decided to make accessible to visitors the funerary chambers ornamented with the famous 'Pyramid Texts' which he had discovered. He entrusted the clearing to Barsanti whom he also charged, from the winter of 1899–1900, with the clearing of the pyramid area so as to locate the enclosure wall and the ruins of the funerary temple that he believed were situated nearby.

*Pls. 60, XV*

In the course of these works, the pretty little mastaba of Samnefer, probably a contemporary of Unas, was uncovered to the north-west of the pyramid,[123] and, to the south, the vast Saite and Persian shafts, several of which had not been penetrated by robbers: those of the chief physician Psamtik and his wife Setaribu,[124] of the Admiral Djenhebu whose mummy was richly adorned with numerous jewels and amulets,[125] and of Pede-ese.[126] In the latter's burial chamber, whose vaulted roof was decorated with raised stars, the inscriptions were brightly coloured and, though each hieroglyph was detailed with great care, Maspero notes[127] that the style does not have the purity found in the finest Saite work. Pede-ese, son of Psamtik, the owner of the adjoining tomb, lived under Darius I and his tomb thus dates from the beginning of the Persian era (end of the sixth and beginning of the fifth century BC).

These three tombs, known as the Persian Tombs, were connected underground by Barsanti who installed a cast-iron spiral staircase in Psamtik's small shaft giving easy access from his chamber to Pede-ese's to the east and Djenhebu's to the west.

In Unas's funerary complex itself, the remains of the walls of his funerary temple were found abutting the eastern side of his pyramid where the base of his stela is still visible; but it was only in the course of the following winter (1900–1) that traces of the great porticoed courtyard were uncovered. A few granite door-sills were still in place as were portions of alabaster paving and, lying on the ground, there were several shattered palm columns in pink granite. There was also an enormous architrave bearing, in large carved hieroglyphs, the royal titles of Unas; it is still in place. Precious fragments of reliefs were scattered about; Barsanti said that he had collected these and put them in a safe place, but did not say where.[128] Then, in the courtyard situated immediately to the north of the temple, there appeared a descending passage leading to a long gallery, eight metres deep, starting as an open trench and continuing as a tunnel in the rock. It was oriented north to south and ran the whole width of the temple. To the east and to the west of this gallery were two other galleries on each side of which, at right-angles, opened fourteen parallel rooms, side by side. Where the main gallery became horizontal it was barred successively by four portcullises with a dozen metres between each. Very long underground chambers opened at right-angles to each side in the intervals between the portcullises and, beyond the fourth portcullis, were the funerary chamber proper and the burial chamber. This underground part of the tomb has a most extensive and complicated design.[129] It also contained, to the east and west, a great number of store-rooms. The systematic exploration of these rooms and stores, which continued throughout the winter of 1901–2, brought to light a vast quantity of vases and dishes in alabaster, diorite and schist, whole or in fragments, and the remains of pottery jars with clay stoppers bearing the seal-impressions of either the Horus Hetep-sekhemwy or the Horus Neb-Re (Raneb), the first two kings of the IInd Dynasty.[130]

This discovery greatly surprised Maspero as no one knew at that time of the existence at Saqqara of large tombs of the Thinite period. It now appears extremely likely that this astonishingly vast warren of subterranean galleries, extending under the temple of Unas, was the funerary complex of the Horus Hetep-sekhemwy whose provisioning was completed and then definitively sealed at the time of his death by officials of Neb-Re, his successor. The superstructure of mud-bricks that must have been built above this underground complex was probably already in ruins before the time of Unas, and finally razed and removed by the latter.[131]

After the work by Maspero and Barsanti, this area of the pyramid of Unas was abandoned for a quarter of a century until C. M. Firth undertook, in December 1929, to complete the clearing of the temple and to search for the fragments of reliefs that Barsanti had hidden. This additional clearing enabled us to establish the ground plan for the major part of the temple with the exception of the store-rooms that extended to the north and south of the entrance vestibule.[132] It was not until the winter of 1936–7, several years after Firth's death, that I was able to clear these and it was only then that we found the reliefs that Barsanti had so carefully concealed: he had in fact placed them, face down, among the paving slabs of the temple.[133]

In the course of the following campaign of 1937–8, Selim Hassan, then Deputy Director-General of the Antiquities Department, put Zakaria Goneim in charge of clearing the deeply buried area that extended to the east of the temple of Unas.[134] Several mastabas were found, the most important being that of the royal son and vizier Neb-kau-hor.[135] It had been usurped by another vizier called Akhet-hetep and contained remains of interesting reliefs inside a vast nine-pillared hall. On the four sides of each pillar, carved in relief, was the standing portrait of the deceased with, above him, his name and titles. Also worthy of mention were the ruins of a small mastaba containing some fine reliefs belonging to Khenu, a priest of the Unas pyramid.

The major discovery, however, was the causeway leading from the valley to the upper temple of the pyramid of Unas.[136] This causeway, more than seven hundred metres long, has a paved way 2·60 m. wide, bordered by the remains of walls built of blocks of Tura limestone. Very few of these remain in place but many others were found lying in the sand all along the causeway. The limestone blocks (some of which were recovered during the campaign of 1940, see p. 153) feature many scenes in relief, including: the transportation of finished granite columns for a funerary temple, lashed to sledges and placed in pairs on barges, from the quarries at Aswan;[137] two ships full of foreign prisoners supplicating the pharaoh; a battle between archers;[138] goldsmiths beating sheets of precious metal, while others, making electrum (an alloy of gold and silver), use blow-pipes to help heat the crucible;[139] a famine scene in which some fifteen starving people are shown in forlorn attitudes;[140] processions of courtiers, etc. There are also market scenes, in one of which two men are seen offering fish, while another man seeks to barter a cake for fresh fish. In an amusing continuation of this scene, a young man exhibits a pet ape to traders and customers, while a piece of furniture is bartered for a basket of fish, the fishmonger extending his hand in a most expressive manner.

In a hunting scene, we see (from right to left) among sand dunes in which grow some cacti, two bucks emerging opposite an oryx which is licking its young; behind it a gazelle is bitten in the leg by a large hunting dog wearing a collar. Then two females arrive at the head of a herd of antelopes; they come to a halt at the sight of the dog and give birth in terror. Above this group other beasts are waking up or rising: from right to left, a gazelle, a jerboa, and a hare. On the upper register, of which only the lower part remains, one can distinguish, behind gazelle

*Pl. XVI*

*Pl. 125*

*Pl. 128*

*Pl. 126*

*Pl. 129*

*Pl. 130*
*Pl. 127*

Pl. XVII

feet, the legs of a hunter followed perhaps by a dog then by a fox with a bushy tail. Behind the latter, one can recognize the relatively thick legs of an ibex or an oryx, followed in turn by a large canine.

Also, just to the south of the causeway, a large dummy boat in stone was uncovered. Hewn in the rock, it was completely encased in fine limestone blocks that rose above ground level. Finally, the vast wall of the Valley Temple was reached from which the causeway starts.

In another sector, immediately to the south of the mastaba of Neb-kau-hor, a shaft preceding a forced portcullis gave access to a whole warren of galleries that contained numerous vases in alabaster and hardstone of the Thinite period, as well as pottery and clay jar sealings with the name of the Horus Neterimu (Neteren) of the IInd Dynasty, making it probable that this was his tomb.[141] Its plan seemed similar to that of the supposed tomb of the Horus Hetep-sekhemwy discovered beneath the temple of Unas about 150 metres further west.

In the summer of 1938 work was interrupted in this sector of the causeway of Unas, but from October 1939 Etienne Drioton, the Director-General of Antiquities, entrusted Zaki Saad with the clearing of the area between the temple and the causeway of Unas and the southern enclosure wall of the Zoser complex.

It was during the course of these works that the huge Saite tomb shaft of General Amen-Tefnakht, sunk within the temple of Unas, was cleared. Inside its intact burial chamber the mummy was found without any jewels or amulets;[142] nevertheless, the tomb proved to be very interesting in its perfect sealing system and the fine quality of the sarcophagus made of greenish schist.

But much more interesting results were obtained in other places. First was the discovery of two mastabas of queens, that of the royal wife Nebet and that of Khenut, perhaps the queen mother.[143] These two adjacent mastabas extend for about fifty metres parallel to the northern face of the Unas temple and a few steps away from it (see Fig. 1). Although the latter is in ruins, the first, belonging to Nebet,[144] presents a nearly complete ground plan including, among other things, a row of double-storied store-houses giving on to a large vestibule decorated with large-size reliefs. Other interesting reliefs were found in the adjoining chambers and a pretty portrait of the queen seated on her throne is carved above the lintel between the first two chambers. The queen is shown sniffing at a lotus flower. Her

Pl. 131

diadem is a wide ribbon tied behind her head and with a long hanging streamer; her jewellery consists of a broad collar and bracelets on her wrists and ankles. She is wearing a long clinging dress with wide shoulder straps which leave the breasts uncovered; this dress has still largely retained its original green colour.

Nearer to Zoser's enclosure wall other mastabas were cleared. They were, starting from the west, the mastaba of Ha-ish-tef who had enlarged the mastaba of his father Ka-i.[145] The main room is situated in the centre of a vast core of mud-brick that presented, on its north side, a fine example of the rolled vault. Next is the mastaba of Inefert,[146] where the scenes on one of its chamber walls are simply drawn and painted. Finally there are the remains of the mastaba of Unas-ankh, its major part having been sold, in 1907, to the Chicago Oriental Institute Museum.

## The Mastaba of Mehu

The most remarkable mastaba in this sector, however, on account of its fine state of preservation is, without doubt, that of the vizier Mehu dating from the beginning of the VIth Dynasty. This mastaba,[147] adjoining Princess Idut's (see p. 77), whose son he seems to have been,[148] owes its having nearly completely escaped the depredations of the stone seekers to its deeper location; it had thus retained the major part of its roof, thanks to which the colours have been preserved in many parts and one can still admire the freshness of their hues and appreciate the skill with which they had been applied.

*Fig. 10*

In the entrance vestibule (Room 1), on the southern wall, are scenes showing the trapping of birds with nets, to be compared with the scenes already described in the mastabas of Kagemni (Plate 48) and of Ptah-hotep (Plate 58). Here also we find trappers who close the nets by throwing themselves backwards, until they are lying flat on their backs in order to heave on the closing ropes at the signal of the chief of operations, who throws his arms out horizontally. Below, other trappers, who have risen, draw a net full of wild duck towards them while some small herons and two ducks have managed to escape. Lower down still, three further trappers, their leader leaning on a long cane and raising his left arm, are dragging along a net in which four storks have been caught, two of these having fallen over, are shown with their legs sticking up in the air; others which have escaped are flying off or preparing to do so. In the bottom register we see the homeward journey with the day's catch; one

*Pl. 132*

X–XII

THE FUNERARY COMPLEX OF ZOSER
X   The restored entrance – the only genuine one, the other fourteen all being dummy portals (cf. p. 99) – of the main enclosure. It leads into the colonnaded entrance hall (cf. Plates 86–8).
   In the background can be seen, rising within the temenos wall, the Step Pyramid.

XI   North Building (cf. p. 134): detail of bell-shaped capitals surmounting the papyrus columns.

XII   South Tomb: relief on the first stela (cf. pp. 96–7). Zoser is shown running in the ritual *heb-sed* race (cf. Plate 100).

X

XI    XII

XIII

XIV

XIII, XIV

of the men is shown carrying a large fowl, already plucked, on his shoulder.

Pl. XIX

In the offerings chamber (Room 4) we see, at the back of this room, Mehu's stela, recording his titles, including those of vizier and of minister of justice. This stela is coloured red-brown to imitate quartzite; on each side of it there are the usual scenes of presentation of offerings, covering the two long north and south walls.

Pl. XX

At the western end of the lowest register of the north wall, the first offering-bearers are shown making a ritual offering to Mehu of geese and storks which they hold by the necks and wings, and which are reacting to this treatment by lifting their feet in very well-observed attitudes. An effort seems to have been made to give depth and modelling to the bodies of these large birds by touches of paint on one side and by some sort of

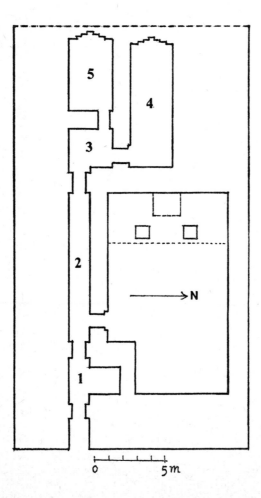

Fig. 10. Plan of the mastaba of Mehu.

gradation or change of colour in places. At the feet of these bearers are cages containing smaller birds: various sorts of duck, pigeons, etc.

In Room 5, later used by an official, Mery-re-ankh, as his offerings chamber, this person is shown, wearing a wide blue collar and bracelets and sitting on a chair with lions'-paw legs, drinking from a cup before the conventional table of offerings to the deceased. Above, on the south wall, reading from right to left, seven columns of hieroglyphs list his titles and inform us that he carried out, among other duties, that of priest of the pyramid of Mery-re (Pepi I); then, over to the right, above the offerings table, the menu with a long list of dishes. Below the inscription a line of standing and kneeling men present offerings. In the lowest register, under Mery-re-ankh's effigy, five bearers present, while bowing respectfully, the legs of sacrificed animals; they are followed by others who are offering pairs of fine geese. All these pictures and hieroglyphs are still vividly coloured, and, although in very low relief, stand out against the greyish-blue background.

*Pl. XVIII*

In Room 5, on the south wall, and forming a continuation of the scene shown in Plate XVIII, we see the edge of the offerings table at the right. In the centre is a fine heap of victuals, which includes trussed geese, a calf's head, quarters of meat, legs of gazelles, baskets of fruits, salads, garnished platters, large vases, etc.; two large goblets of veined stone are each surmounted by an artistically tied and knotted ribbon. Below, the file of offering-bearers, still nicely coloured, is particularly meticulously drawn and varied in its details.

*Pl. 133*

On the east wall is a notable scene showing the felling of a fine ox with lyre-shaped horns and large black spot-markings.

*Pl. 134*

The clearing of the causeway of Unas was not resumed until 1940 when Etienne Drioton entrusted the work to the architect Abdel-Salam Mohammed Hussein who had been my assistant from the beginning of 1938 until the outbreak of war when, mobilized in France, I had been unable to rejoin the Antiquities Department.

Since the royal causeway, sloping down towards the valley, disappeared beneath a considerable amount of sand and debris, Abdel-Salam preferred first to check its course by making soundings in the bottom of the wadi that it should normally be following. He was thus able, after having established that the causeway changed its course some 320 metres from the Valley

Temple's great western wall, to determine its course with precision.[149] He then started methodically to clear towards the east from the point where Selim Hassan and Zakaria Goneim had stopped. Pieces of paving slabs were still in place, some remains of the first course of the side walls and a certain number of scattered blocks with carved reliefs were discovered. Among these was the impressively realistic famine scene already referred to (see p. 145).

The removal of the sand from between the causeway and the rocky plateau it skirts, revealed several more tombs. The most interesting of these is that of Ptah-iru-ka, 'Chief of the roads of the slaughterhouse', who is represented ten times in the tomb, carved in the rock in high relief, stuccoed and painted; the colours on these figures, as well as on the accompanying hieroglyphs, are still very vivid. A number of very beautiful wooden statues were also discovered in an adjoining tomb of a certain Akhti-hetep.[150]

*Pl. 135*

### The Mastaba of Nefer-her-Ptah

About ten metres away from this tomb is a mastaba placed at right-angles to the causeway, which covers its northern face, nearly blocking its entrance. Built for a certain Nefer-her-Ptah shortly before the accession of Unas, it was unfinished; the cutting of the scenes had been interrupted because of the threat of expropriation for the construction of the royal causeway. But the drawings had been done with extreme care and, in some places, coloured.

*Pl. 136*

The scenes on the western wall show a flock of birds, drawn and painted with a remarkable degree of accuracy and skill, some of which (in the central portion) have been caught in a hexagonal net, while those that have managed to escape are rapidly flying away. Another scene shows a huntsman bringing in his catch and delivering it to two assistants who are putting the birds into cages; several other birds are standing on top of the cages with their wings tied. Gardeners are also depicted, replanting or gathering vegetables, in a scene which includes a large basketful of various fruits (melons, grapes, pomegranates), vegetables and lotus flowers.

*Pl. 137*

*Pl. 138*

The scenes carved at the northern end of this register also show the gathering of grapes from vines grown on trellises, with the vintagers delicately taking hold of the bunches with the thumb and forefinger, and six others treading the grapes in a vat. In this scene they hold on to a horizontal bar above their

*Pl. 139*

*Pl. 140*

heads with one hand and with the other grasp each other by the waist, forming two facing groups so as to maintain rhythmic time, provided by two men using small sticks or some sort of castanets (not shown in the illustration).

On the northern wall, amid scenes depicting craftsmen at work and cattle farming, we see a miscreant servant being beaten in the presence of an overseer, who watches the scene leaning on the head of his cane. The man meting out the punishment is using a switch of which, due to the deterioration of the edges of the stone, only one of the ends shows in his palm.

*Pl. 141*

During the winter of 1943–4, Abdel-Salam, who had undertaken the clearing of the Valley Temple of Unas, made an unexpected discovery; after having found the corner of a terrace with a parapet reached by a ramp, and uncovered the base of a granite palm column lying nearby, he was greatly surprised to find a superb sarcophagus made of white-veined grey schist. It was lying on the paving near the base of a destroyed wall against which it must have been placed.[151] It was decorated with small ribboned torus mouldings on the four vertical corners as well as on the outside horizontal edges of its rim, very similar to the sarcophagus of Mycerinus from Giza that was lost at sea while in transit to London.[152] Like it, also, this newly discovered example had a lid whose edge was cornice-shaped. The slightly displaced lid bore, on one of its corners, traces of the tools that had been used to force it open. Inside there was a badly damaged mummy bathed in a reddish amber liquid that filled the sarcophagus nearly to the brim. The mummy had obviously been despoiled of its principal finery and of part of its wrappings. Nevertheless, to the left of the detached and turned skull, there still remained some scraps of wrinkled gold-leaf and, on the waist, a gold belt with coloured beads. It was practically intact in the midst of this rotting mess. Lastly, there was a large ovoid cornelian bead threaded on a gold wire wrapped four times around the right wrist, and a gold band wrapped around the same arm beneath the elbow. The presence of these few precious remnants proved that the robbers had to act quickly and leave before they could complete their work. The replacement of the lid in its grooves and its closure was certainly not done by the robbers; it seems more likely to indicate that it was an attempt to restore the burial after its violation.

The belt found in these strange circumstances is a remarkable jewel as much for its beauty and fine craftsmanship as for its archaeological value. It is a gold band with a trimming of beads: 'Beads of gold, blue and black stones form a geometric design of multi-coloured squares fixed by their edges. A notched gold plaque breaks this design in the middle of the back. Its purpose was to hang the imitation bull's tail that was part of the belts of kings and gods . . .' – such was Drioton's description.[153] He also pointed out that King Narmer wears a similar belt on his famous Palette.

The belt had a gold clasp inlaid with coloured pieces forming a symmetrical design representing twice, face to face, the owner of the jewel. He is seated on a throne holding a long staff and wearing a loincloth finely chiselled on the gold of the plaque; a royal *uraeus* is on his forehead. A falcon, its wings at right-angles, is flying towards him holding the seal in its talons above the engraved hieroglyphs that give the name and titles of the deceased: 'The prince, son of the king, Ptah-shepses.'[154] Who was he? Probably a son of Unas. His nearby mastaba must have been desecrated and therefore his sarcophagus was placed for safe-keeping in one of the chambers of the lower temple, by priests of the funeral rites of the king, until the mastaba could be restored.

Excavations in this Valley Temple had now to be stopped because they had reached the present access road to the necropolis. While waiting for the authorities to re-route this road, Abdel-Salam transferred his excavations, first to the southern part of Saqqara to the pyramid called 'Haram esh-Shawaf' (the 'Pyramid of the Watcher') that dominates the village and whose owner had not yet been identified, and on to the Bent Pyramid of Dahshur in 1946.

At the Haram esh-Shawaf, Abdel-Salam started simultaneously to open the pyramid and to clear its funerary temple. He quickly succeeded in achieving his aim, which was to identify the owner of this funerary complex. Fragments of reliefs in the temple soon revealed the name of King Isesy Djed-ka-re of the Vth Dynasty, the immediate predecessor of Unas. The burial chamber had no inscriptions on the walls, so Unas must have been the first king to have the principal rooms of his tomb carved with the famous 'Pyramid Texts'.

*Pls. 60, XV*

After Abdel-Salam's premature death in the United States during a visit there in 1949, no more work was done in the Unas complex except for some sporadic digging. Nevertheless, this enabled the architect Hilmy Basha to uncover a second dummy boat adjoining the first, and part of the same fine limestone masonry mass that marks their outline.

*Pl. XVII*

Attempts to restore the causeway between 1954 and 1960 had to be abandoned because no preliminary study had been made. However, during that period Awad Raslan was able to replace, on the southern face of the pyramid, the fragments of the inscription of Prince Kha-em-wase which I had discovered in 1937, and to re-erect the granite palm column at the entrance to the Valley Temple.

It was only during 1965 to 1967 that more important work could be carried out on the Unas causeway. This enabled the two Antiquities Department inspectors, Mounir Basta and Ahmed Musa, who were successively in charge, to uncover, immediately to the south of the causeway, numerous tombs, two of which are quite remarkable and are described below. The first was reached by Mounir Basta while clearing the shaft of a Late Period tomb. This shaft went through the rock-cut offerings chamber of a Vth Dynasty tomb whose original entrance had been blocked from the time of Unas when he built his causeway, and therefore must belong to an earlier period than the causeway.

*Hypogeum and Mastaba of Khnum-hetep and Ni-ankh-khnum*
Found full of bones and mummies of Roman times, this tomb is curious in that it belonged to two people, perhaps twin brothers – Khnum-hetep and Ni-ankh-khnum – who are represented in painted relief, each accompanied by his son, on either side of the entrance to the first rock-hewn chamber. Inside, the two brothers are represented embracing side by side, sometimes nose to nose. Among the titles quoted on their stelae, or on the wall scenes, are 'Chief of the court manicurists' and 'Priest of the solar temple of Ni-user-re' (the fifth or sixth king of the Vth Dynasty).

*Pl. 142*

On the southern part of the western wall, we see (to the left, in the lowest register), boatmen jousting with their boat-hooks, and (to the right) a boat being punted along, laden with poultry and lotus flowers. In the second register, a herd of cattle is crossing a ford, preceded by two papyrus boats laden with provisions. The movements of the heads of the cattle with their big lyre-shaped horns are most artistically composed.

*Pl. 143*

In the third register, we see (from left to right): a herdsman quartering a gazelle hung by its hind legs, then, in front of an old man with pointed beard and hollow stomach who leans on a long cane, a cow being milked; the latter is preceded by its calf and by a farmhand who is watering a young ox by means of a large bowl. Finally, to the right, a cow is shown calving and, while one cow-hand is holding it firmly by the horns, another grasps the new-born calf by the head and legs (cf. the very similar scene in the mastaba of Ti, Plate 21).

In the upper register, men are preparing loaves of bread and passing them to the baker standing in front of his oven; to the right an overseer watches two men seated face to face with small brushes, who are cleaning papyrus fibres, while a third, sitting comfortably in a low seat, weaves them.[155]

### Hypogeum of Nefer

The second tomb, discovered a year later by Ahmed Musa, is in a remarkable state of preservation, including its colouring. It consists of a single oblong accessible chamber that widens towards the east at its southern extremity. In its floor are the funerary shafts of five men and women. The most important of these bears the name of Nefer.[156] The western wall is nearly completely covered by the two stelae of Nefer (at the end towards the south), that of his wife Khonsu, and also by the stelae of several members of his family. Another stela is that of Urbau, wearing a panther-skin, and of his wife Khent-kaus; they are shown seated, face to face, at a table towards which each extends a hand.

At the end of the room, on the southern wall, we can see Nefer standing with his wife sitting at his feet, while in front of them, in the bottom register, two musicians are playing harps.

On the eastern wall, in its northern section, the scene in the lower register shows a farmer guiding a plough drawn by two oxen driven by a herdsman wielding a stick. In front of them a peasant is sowing grain which is being trampled into the earth by a flock of rams flanked by two shepherds.

Except for, on the extreme right, the two groups of dwarfs making necklaces, the scene in the second register is concerned with the grape harvest: four vintagers, holding on to each other by one hand round the waist and to a bar with the other, are treading grapes in a vat to the rhythm of two men beating small sticks together (cf. Plates 57 and 140). Behind these men are large jars and amphorae for storing the wine and, to the far left, the grape-pressing scene like that in the mastaba of Ptah-hotep (Plate 57), but here with an amusing detail. The man who, in Ptah-hotep's mastaba, was stretched out horizontally to heave

*Pl. 144*

*Pl. 145*

against the two poles that had to be separated completely in order to squeeze the last drops of juice from the grapes inside the bag tied between them, is here replaced by a trained baboon, which seems to carry out its duties with great ease.

On the same wall, slightly more to the south, there is, in the bottom register, a particularly animated scene of men battling on water. Between the two first boats, from the left, one of the pole-wielders has been thrown into the water; another, balancing on the prow of the fourth boat, is about to be thrown in.

*Pl. 146*

In the second register, Nefer's wife is seen sitting under a pergola, with small lotiform columns, from which provisions are hanging. She appears to be clasping a baby to her breast while another, slightly older child, holds her hand. In front of this group, four dancers are dancing a graceful sylvan ballet for which three accompanists are beating time by clapping. Behind these advances a file of offering-bearers advances.

In the third register, the preparation and baking of bread over an open fire, followed by a hunter, whose net has trapped a group of ducks on a pond, is putting his catch in two cages carried by a man with a yoke. A second hunter is carrying, tied to a pole over his shoulder, his hunting knives and lasso, and several birds hung by their legs from a cord.

In the upper register a small herd, led by a herdsman with his water-jug and blanket over his shoulder, emerges from a papyrus marsh; then, watched by an overseer leaning on his long stick, a second herdsman endeavours to make a young ox drink from a large bowl that he holds, by pushing its head down into it; above, another young ox, tethered to a hoop driven into the ground, is waiting its turn. Behind the overseer, finally, a servant leaning against a clump of papyrus seems to be scouring out a bowl.

The desiccated body of one of the occupants of the tomb was covered, according to the technique used during most of the Old Kingdom, with a sort of doll-like linen wrapping upon which all the details of the face, the body and the limbs had been modelled and painted. It lay in its coffin holding, in one hand, a *kherep* sceptre and, in the other, a long stick; they are both of wood and well preserved.

Work now being carried out in this area has uncovered, beneath the foundation of the causeway of Unas, all the lower courses of a mastaba built for Khnum-hotep and Ni-ankh-khnum; the previously discovered hypogeum was only its southern edge. Also, by a fortunate and very exceptional chance, practically every one of the relief-decorated blocks taken from this mastaba had been re-used in the foundations of the causeway. These blocks were carefully sorted out and studied by Ahmed Musa and Dr H. Altenmüller, of the German Archaeological Institute in Cairo, before being put back in place in the mastaba whose reconstruction was undertaken. This has now been carried out with great success by the chief architect of the Antiquities Department, Yakoub Memdou, and the whole of this very fine mastaba is now accessible to tourists.

### The Memphite Tomb of Horemheb

A joint archaeological expedition, directed by Dr Geoffrey T. Martin, and sponsored by the Egypt Exploration Society of London and the National Museum of Antiquities, Leyden, discovered in January 1975 the Memphite tomb of the Horemheb in an area south of the Unas Causeway at Saqqara. Horemheb, a great official of Tutankhamun and of Ay, himself ascended the throne as king, *c.* 1335 BC. His tomb, intended for him as a private person, was still in the process of decoration at the time of his accession. A fine tomb, also unfinished, was prepared for him in the Valley of the Kings at Thebes.

The Saqqara tomb, which is entered from the east, consists of a large open courtyard with papyriform columns, with a main central chapel at the west end, flanked by vaulted chambers. Many of the fine reliefs from the walls of the tomb had been removed in antiquity and in modern times during the early decades of the nineteenth century; others were found *in situ* by the recent expedition, while more were found loose in the debris of the tomb.

# The IVth Dynasty 'Mastabat Fara'un',
# the VIth Dynasty Funerary Complex of Pepi II,
# and Two Pyramids of the XIIIth Dynasty

From 1924 to 1936, while C. M. Firth, followed by J. E. Quibell and myself, were making the discoveries described in preceding chapters in the northern sector of Saqqara, excavation of an important area in the southern sector had, in 1924, been entrusted by the Director-General of the Antiquities Department to Gustave Jéquier. This Swiss Egyptologist had first concentrated on the curious monument called, by the local inhabitants, the 'Mastabat Fara'un', which means 'the seat of the pharaoh'. Its descending corridor, previously opened by Mariette, was again completely blocked by sand. While emptying it to gain access to the fine granite-vaulted chambers in the interior, Jéquier cleared the area surrounding the visible structure that was built of enormous courses of fossil-bearing local limestone. He soon discovered a few of the fine Tura limestone casing blocks that must have covered the building above a lower course in granite. This enabled him to deduce that its original exterior shape had been that of an immense sarcophagus with an arched top (see Fig. 11).[157] He then cleared the whole monumental complex including the remains of a funerary temple whose walls, except for three granite blocks remaining in place, had disappeared. It had been set against the eastern face of the main structure. In this temple's paved courtyard were found fragments of a royal statue in dolerite, and on one of these fragments was the lower part of a cartouche showing that the last letter of the king's name was an *f* preceded by the corner of another sign that must have been a *ka*. Jéquier also found, in the immediate vicinity, a Middle Kingdom relief on which a certain Ptah-hotep boasts of having re-established the cult of King Shepseskaf. He therefore concluded that it was logical to attribute the 'Mastabat Fara'un' to this king of the IVth Dynasty, the son of Mycerinus.[158]

A large courtyard bounded by a mud-brick panelled wall lay in front of the temple and two mud-brick enclosures surrounded the complex that was joined to the still-buried Valley Temple by a mud-brick ramp at least 760 metres in length. This causeway, only 1·70 m. wide, was roofed and roughly plastered without

*Pl. 147*

*Pl. 148*

decoration. There was nothing sumptuous about this causeway and Jéquier supposed that it had been built in haste after the king's death.

### The Funerary Complex of Pepi II

Pl. 149

The main object of work in this sector was the clearing of the vast funerary complex of Pepi II with its small satellite pyramid,[159] and the three pyramids of his queens, Udjebten,[160] Neith and Ipuit.[161] From the point of view of its plan, the complex of Pepi II is the most complete royal monument from the VIth Dynasty discovered at Saqqara (see Fig. 12). It enabled important gaps existing in the remains of the temples of Unas and Teti to be interpreted. Of the relief scenes Jéquier has re-incorporated many fragments on some of the walls of the temple where sufficient evidence remained for a definitive reconstruction; other scenes have been tentatively reconstructed by him on the basis of fragmentary evidence. These scenes are valuable additions to the art of the period, previously known mainly through Borchardt's explorations at the Vth Dynasty pyramids of Abusir.[162] All these reliefs are executed in a very fine style.

It was from Pepi II's pyramid itself that Jéquier got the most remarkable results. Having undertaken to clear the funerary chambers ravaged by the stone robbers of the Middle Ages who, looking for fine limestone blocks, had exploited the text-covered walls of the two central chambers, he collected from among the mass of debris a large number of inscribed fragments. Copying and carefully studying these fragments in order to identify the 'Pyramid Texts' chapters to which they belonged, he was later able to restore the majority to their original place on the walls that he had rebuilt for this purpose.

Pl. 150

Fig. 11. Reconstruction of the 'Mastabat Fara'un'. After Jéquier and Lauer.

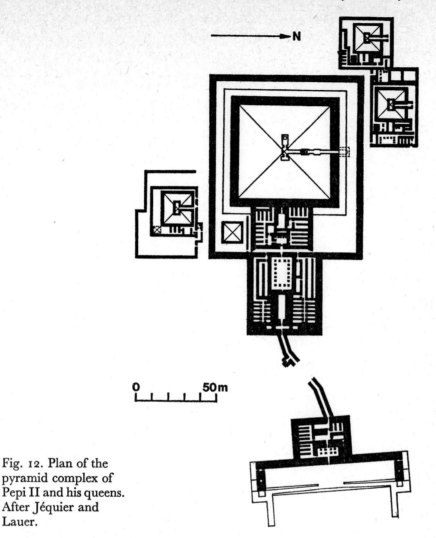

Fig. 12. Plan of the
pyramid complex of
Pepi II and his queens.
After Jéquier and
Lauer.

The walls of the burial chambers in the three pyramids of
Pepi II's queens were also covered with partly preserved
'Pyramid Texts', to which the excavations made some useful
additions.[163] Lastly, not far from the temple of Pepi II, a few
steps to the south of its causeway, Jéquier discovered the small,
much-destroyed pyramid of King Haka-re Aba (or Ibi), probably of the VIIIth Dynasty, which also contained texts.[164]

These excavations at southern Saqqara have thus given us an
important harvest of fragments of texts that have been added to
those published first by Maspero and then by K. Sethe. Joined
to those that, as we shall see, will continue to appear in the
course of our present excavations, they will form an important

mass of supplementary documents that will necessitate a more complete edition of the 'Pyramid Texts' in a new form more suited to the present needs of Egyptology.

While carrying out this work in the funerary complex of Pepi II, Jéquier explored several tombs of courtiers of the king and also tombs of those of lesser rank.[165] These tombs always consisted of a burial chamber oriented north to south and an access shaft entering the room from the north side. Depths vary from two to twelve metres, the shallower tombs being the poorer ones. In the more important tombs, the burial chamber is lined with limestone and is roofed with slabs of the same material; the ceiling slabs are protected by a relieving vault in crude bricks, which were sometimes arranged in voussoirs when the tomb was deep; in such cases the vault was often doubled or even tripled. Often the walls of the chamber were covered with decorations appropriate to what was considered necessary for life in the hereafter. Usually this decoration was cut in very low relief and painted, sometimes only painted. Scenes covered the walls above two yellow and red bands that delimit the black painted dado of the room. They are topped by a hieroglyphic inscription whose object was to obtain from a divinity, through the king, a material favour in the next world.

On the eastern wall the prayer is made to Osiris, as Lord of Busiris and Master of Abydos who, as god of vegetation and resurrection, has to supply the dead man with food. Thus the first scene from the entrance consists of a still-life in which all the offerings are represented in great detail and brightly coloured.[166] This scene is completed by the general list of foods that took its final shape towards the end of the IVth Dynasty. 'It is an intangible text', wrote Jéquier,[167] 'of a religious and ritualistic order possessing a magical strength by virtue of a formula and whose presence only in a tomb takes the place, for ever, of prayers and ceremonies destined to provide for the upkeep of the deceased.'

Then comes the offerings niche, painted in bright colours, that symbolizes the monumental entrance of the royal palace. Here we have an affirmation that the deceased is lodged in the king's palace and that he can, from the depths of his tomb, partly at least, enjoy the latter's privileges. One notices how generally, in the history of ancient Egyptian funerary dogma, a rite originally intended for the king alone, reverts little by little to general use when, by virtue of its formula, it acts for the ordinary man as it does for the king. In addition, via the niche in which is represented a false door, the *ka* can go out and resume contact with the world of the living.

The narrower, southern panel is, generally, only an extension to the store-rooms and upon it is often represented granaries and heaps of dried fruit.

On the western wall is located an invocation to Anubis, the god 'that is on the mountain, in the Libyan desert, the master of the sacred earth'. He is asked to ensure that the dead man receives a good burial in his tomb. This does not mean perishable foodstuffs, but objects represented and accompanied by their names, arranged upon low tables.[168] Starting from the entrance one sees: the seven sacred oils or essences, represented by the hardstone or elaborate vases in various shapes that contained them, and accompanied by two kinds of make-up represented by small skin bags; then come the sets of jewels (necklaces, bracelets and belts) that formed the official dress of the deceased followed by those of clothes differentiated mainly by their names; finally, various objects, such as incense tablets for ritual censing, the sandals, the head-rest, the scribe's palette and the ewer for ablutions, complete the picture, in the centre of which a polychrome false door faces the niche in the opposite wall.

The coffins were of wood, rectangular and with flat lids. An inscription in large incised and blue-painted hieroglyphs usually runs along the top of the outer faces of the coffin and down the middle of its lid; it gave the deceased's name, together with the usual ritual formula. Sometimes an embellishment of very thin gold-leaf covers the corners of the box.

Inside the canopic chests, also in wood, no traces of the expected vases were found. Jéquier therefore surmised that, for reasons of economy, it was found sufficient merely to put in the cases the four parcels containing the viscera taken from the mummy of the deceased.

The owners of these tombs did not possess any good statues of their 'double', or *ka*; they were satisfied with hardwood statuettes at most 0·25 m. high, sometimes consisting of fairly small pieces of sculpture, certainly not *objets d'art*. Other figurines, rougher and daubed in red paint, represented servants at work or sailors.

Since all these tombs had been robbed, very few objects or jewels were found. Of the provisions themselves nothing remained except for the pots or dishes in which they had been stored but, to compensate for this, some models of meat and fowls of carved and painted stone were brought to light.[169]

XV–XVII

XV

XVI

XVII

XVIII

XIX

XX

XVIII–XX

THE MASTABA OF THE VIZIER MEHU

XVIII  Room 5, later used by an official – Mery-re-ankh – as his offerings chamber. He is depicted, sitting before the conventional table of offerings, drinking from a cup (cf. p. 153).

XIX  Room 4, the offerings chamber (cf. p. 152). At the back of this room can be seen Mehu's stela, coloured red-brown to imitate quartzite. Mehu held the titles, among others, of vizier and minister of justice.

XX  Room 4, the offerings chamber, west end of the north wall. The first bearers making a ritual offering of geese and storks to Mehu (cf. p. 152).

Some more important tombs belonging to high dignitaries of the reign of Pepi II, but generally greatly ravaged by robbers, were also cleared by Jéquier. They consist of nearly square mastabas with sides up to twenty-five metres long, their massive core being partitioned by dividing walls and held together by thick walls made of small stones and clay-mortar. They must have been encased in fine limestone which has since completely disappeared. The access to the burial chamber, similar to those we have described but larger, was not through a vertical shaft but down an incline. In the middle of the western wall of the chamber the monolithic sarcophagus was placed beneath the paving of a large niche, and in the eastern wall a small door opened on to a *serdab*.

Inside these tombs, on the eastern side, traces were found of chapels with many rooms, one of which contained a large false door. Sometimes a place of worship seems to have been installed on the actual terrace of the mastaba. Moreover, the mastaba of the vizier and royal prince Teti had, at the head of its inclined entrance, a small chapel with a stela and offerings table, as in the royal pyramids, and two small obelisks standing in front of the door of the chapel.

Among the objects left behind by the robbers was a very fine statue in hardwood and in a good state of preservation, 0·86 m. high, found in the rubble of the mastaba of Ama-merire; but as its base, on which would have been inscribed this minister's name and titles, is missing we cannot be sure that this statue belonged to him.[170]

Having finished his researches in the inscribed pyramids, Jéquier transferred his workmen about one kilometre further south to a point where there were the remains of two nearly flattened pyramids that had already been noticed by de Morgan, who had marked them on his map.[171] The northernmost one still shows some crude brick courses arranged in regular horizontal layers forming a mass forty-two metres square. But the fine limestone casing had disappeared except for a few fragments, some of which gave the angle of its slope. Jéquier was thus able to calculate that this pyramid had a base of nearly fifty metres and a height of about thirty-five metres.

Although the monument's superstructure had been so terribly destroyed, its funerary chambers were, by contrast, very well preserved (see Fig. 13). The entrance ramp, starting slightly to the south of the middle of the western face, has steps in its centre to allow the funeral procession to descend with ease while the coffin slid down on the ramps on either side of the steps. After a few metres of steep incline, the ramp reaches a landing blocked by a wall 1·30 m. high, at which point a large quartzite port-cullis, weighing about fifteen tons, was intended, after the funeral, to close the passage by sliding across it; but this port-cullis was never used. Beyond, the passage continues, less steeply, for a dozen metres until a second landing is reached, blocked by another 1·30 m. high wall and another lateral port-cullis that, similarly, had never been used. The passage then proceeds with only a slight incline until it reaches a square chamber that seems to be the end of the funerary rooms. But, 1·10 m. beneath its paving, there was a small passage, a tunnel beneath the masonry, leading northwards at right-angles and emerging, seven metres further on, into an oblong antechamber oriented east to west and on the same level. Towards the middle of this antechamber, and at a lower level, another passage leads southwards and reaches the burial chamber; it consists of an enormous quartzite monolith inside which spaces had been hollowed out to take, respectively, the mummy, the canopic chest and the funerary furniture. The access passage opens on to the two huge transverse blocks that form the roof; the first of these had to be raised and supported until the king had been buried inside. Two quartzite props, fitted into hollow shafts partly filled with sand, took the weight of the block, which could then be gently lowered when the sand was allowed to pour out of the base of the shafts. This system, which had been used for the first time in the pyramid of Amenemhet III at Hawara (some sixty-five kilometres south-west of Saqqara), occurred again, as will be seen, in the second pyramid discovered by Jéquier as well as at the one of Mazghuna, south of Dahshur. Here it had functioned perfectly and the roof fitted snugly over the burial chamber. Because of the hardness of quartzite, the tomb-robbers were only able to cut a small hole in the chamber, barely large enough to admit a child; but as nothing at all was found inside, one wonders whether it had ever been occupied. In addition, above the ceiling blocks of the burial chamber, gigantic roofing slabs forming an inverted 'V' acted as a reliev-ing vault beneath the mass of the pyramid.

About eight metres away from this last pyramid an enclosure wall in fine limestone had been removed by stone robbers and nothing remained except a few scattered blocks to show that it had been decorated with bastions and panels.[172] The temple, situated to the east, had also been destroyed and is only marked out by the remains of its basement built of large blocks. On some fragments of fine limestone casing and pieces of palm-shaped columns Jéquier found cartouches of Userkare Khendjer, a king of the XIIIth Dynasty, previously known only from the royal papyrus in the Turin Museum and from two scarabs. He also found, on the pyramid's northern face, traces of a small chapel like the ones built, during the Old Kingdom and at the beginning of the XIIth Dynasty, over the entrance to the descending corridor. As the corridor in this instance started from a completely different point (the western face), one can see how the old tradition of a north chapel has nevertheless been retained.

The most important discovery made amidst the debris of this chapel was that of fragments, in fine-grained black granite, of the apex-stone of a pyramid, the restoration of which was not possible.[173] It is of the same type as the one found by de Morgan in front of the pyramid of Amenemhet at Dahshur and was covered with interesting inscriptions giving useful information on the funerary doctrines of the Middle Kingdom: 'The unity of the whole,' wrote Jéquier,[174] 'is symbolically asserted by the presence, at the summit of the four sides, beneath the extreme point, of a solar disc lowering its wings to protect overall the sovereign buried under the pyramid . . .' On the east face, towards the rising sun, the two solar barques of day and night are face to face, allowing the passing of the sun from one to the other; above them are the gods of morning and of night, Re and Atum, who are taking over the protection of the king, represented by his divine name. The inscription adds: 'The opening of the face of King Userkare, so that he may contemplate the Master of the Horizon, and cross the heavens; that Khendjer may appear as the Master of Eternity, indestructible . . .' On the west face, it is Anubis who looks after the king in Amenti, where he reigns and where he is asked to 'receive Khendjer with open arms, to make him enter into the land of the west, in the sanctuary of the Master of Offerings, where it is pleasant'. On the north side is the world of stars welcoming the king, while, on the south, Ptah, the god of Memphis, assures him of stability and power. In addition, a truncated bust of a royal statuette in black granite that was found nearby must represent Khendjer.[175]

The outline of a second enclosure wall, measuring 122 × 126 m., but built of crude brick, not stone, now appeared. In the

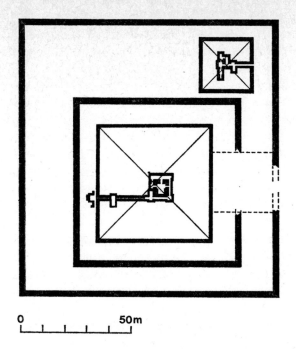

Fig. 13. Plan of the pyramid of Khendjer. After Jéquier and Lauer.

0       50m

northern zone of this area, three great shafts led to underground rooms with insecure and ruined walls; they contained quartzite sarcophagi somewhat rough and in bad condition, which do not appear to have been occupied and which, doubtless, were destined for members of the royal family.

In the north-eastern corner of this second enclosure, Jéquier cleared the remains of a small pyramid, twenty-five metres square, whose core of crude brick and casing of stone had almost completely disappeared but whose interior arrangements were practically intact. The entrance passage, with steps and lateral ramps, is situated in the middle of the eastern base. It continues as a horizontal passage, blocked by two portcullises similar to those in the royal pyramid, till it reaches an ante-chamber giving access to two small tomb chambers, one to the north and the other to the south (each with its canopic chest), that had never been occupied, though the two portcullises in the passage were closed. This pyramid, probably built for queens, had, like that of Khendjer, never been used. This king of the XIIIth Dynasty, the sixteenth to reign after the extinction of the XIIth Dynasty, ruled for at least four years, according to graffiti on blocks of stone; perhaps, in those troubled times, he had been dethroned, and was thus unable to make use of the tombs prepared for himself and for members of his family.

About a hundred metres further south a slight hillock of a darker colour than the surrounding sand marked the location of the second royal monument of the same type, but larger. The main core, built of crude bricks, a few courses of which still remained, measured eighty metres square and the pyramid, with its casing, that was perhaps never fitted, should have measured about ten metres more at the base. At the centre of the core, an enormous shaft dug by robbers had laid bare the pointed roof of huge slabs that formed a relieving vault above the burial chamber. The interior arrangements of this pyramid, analogous to that of Khendjer (Fig. 13), are quite remarkable; the plan is, in fact, the most elaborate and the most complete that had ever been devised by the Egyptian architects to ensure the inviolability of a pyramid. Three large portcullises set at some distance apart were meant successively to bar the way to and, at the same time, hide the access passage to the burial chamber; each time this passage continued (as with Khendjer) beyond the level of the roof, while certain rooms or dead-end passages were built to mislead any possible robbers. After the last portcullis (see Fig. 14) the passage leads into the centre of an antechamber placed at right-angles to it and whose paving is raised, on each side, to a height of 1·10 m. On the left side a small flight of steps allows easy access to this higher level. Towards the north-eastern corner of the antechamber a few steps northward lead to a slightly oblique passage, 4·05 m. long, at the end of which lies the sarcophagus sunk into the paving and flanked by a cavity on the east for the canopic chest; the lid is stored just beyond, slightly inclined, ready to be drawn over the sarcophagus at the right moment. This would have set in motion a lateral portcullis that, sliding into place, was supposed to lock the lid on top of the sarcophagus. But the fact that this lid was still poised in readiness is evidence that the tomb had never been used. Jéquier thinks that it was for the queen; one can, however, object that if her burial was to take place after that of the king, this would have been very dangerous for the safety of the royal mummy, because until the queen died the blocking mechanism of the passage and the activating of the three portcullises could not occur. One can, therefore, wonder if this also was not a dummy burial chamber built in order to mislead robbers, or even a symbolic tomb for the king which, instead of being situated in a small satellite pyramid as it would have been during the Old Kingdom or at the beginning of the XIIth Dynasty, is here incorporated in the main pyramid.

Quartzite

Granite

Limestone

Sand

**section AB**

Fig. 14. Section and plan showing access to and method of closing burial chamber in the unfinished XIIIth Dynasty pyramid. Key: *a*, temporary support; *b*, prop; *c*, sand-filled sheath; *d*, plug to release sand; *e*, working chamber; *f*, roof slabs; *g*, access passage to working chamber; *h*, portcullis; *i*, space for canopic chest; *j*, burial chamber; *k*, access to second vault.

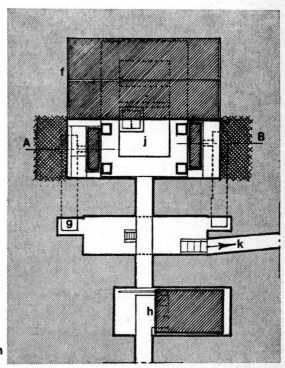

0          5m

175

The king's proper burial chamber is just beyond the ante-chamber in the axis of the access passage (see Fig. 14), which reaches it at the level of its roof, made of enormous juxtaposed quartzite blocks, the first of which is still raised in a waiting position, thus proving that the pyramid had not been used even though one of the portcullises had functioned, perhaps accidentally. The room itself is cut within a quartzite monolith of colossal proportions (6·20 × 4·25 m. and 2·80 m. high) which, before being hollowed out, must have weighed at least 185 tons. The hollowed-out spaces for the burial and for the canopic chest are carved in the mass (just as with Khendjer), and there was also the small bench carrying the lid, as for a sarcophagus, itself still inside, and a large space for offerings and funerary furniture. One cannot but admire the consummate skill of the builders who succeeded in placing there, at the bottom of a vast pit a dozen metres deep, this huge monolith that still weighed, even after being hollowed out, over a hundred tons, and who were able to orient and level it with such perfect precision. A second, equally remarkable, feat would have been the one intended, but not carried out, of lowering in place the large monolith weighing forty-five tons comprising the burial chamber's roof; two quartzite props, their bases fitting in sand-filled sheaths, supported the block. These props would lower it gently down as they slowly sank into the sheaths, when the sand they contained was allowed to pour out by unblocking the openings in their bases (see Fig. 14).

Nothing remains of the temple of this pyramid and it does not seem even to have been started, but the outline of an enclosure wall is clearly marked by the presence of a sinusoidal crude brick wall that could only have been built as a protection against the encroaching sand until it could be replaced by a definitive enclosure in stone masonry.

Jéquier considered that this monument could not be prior to Khendjer and proposed to attribute it tentatively to his successor Semenkhkare-Mermenfitu. 'The name Mermenfitu,' he wrote,[176] 'is not really a name but a military title that can be translated as "general", which seems to indicate that he was an usurper rather than a legitimate king; of this ruler we have only the two colossal statues, found at Tanis, that indicate that he was a powerful monarch with a taste for grandiose achievements and who ruled over the northern part of Egypt at least . . .'

# New Explorations at the VIth Dynasty Pyramids Concerning the 'Pyramid Texts'

The inscribed 'Pyramid Texts', referred to earlier, are the most ancient mythological, religious and literary writings known in Egypt. Very varied in origin and character, they were assembled by the priests of Heliopolis in order to assist the deceased king in his peregrinations around the cosmic circuit. They are ritual and religious texts that were supposed to act by the magical strength of the written words and enable the king's soul to triumph over all the obstacles of the hereafter. The king's odyssey after his death is here, in some way, traced out, culminating in a real apotheosis at Re's side, with whom he would be thenceforth closely associated. These texts are therefore highly interesting, not only for the interpretation of beliefs concerning the survival of the pharaoh in the abode of the sun-god Re and his connection with Osiris and the various other gods, but also for the study of Egyptian writing, language and syntax. They show, in fact, a stage of development of the language generally much older than the inscriptions in the mastabas of the IVth and Vth Dynasties.

That is why, confronted with remarkable results relating to these texts obtained by Jéquier, Pierre Lacau, then Director-General of Antiquities, immediately realized the importance of clearing and exploring the three other pyramids of the VIth Dynasty – those of Teti, Pepi I and Merenre – whose interior chambers, like those of Pepi II, revealed texts and had been ravaged by stone robbers in the Middle Ages. Unfortunately, exhausted by the heavy duties he had assumed during two decades, Lacau had to retire in the spring of 1936 and return to France without being able to put his project into effect. About fifteen years were to pass before his disciple and friend, Jean Sainte Fare Garnot, whose interest in the subject had been aroused, could mount an expedition and obtain the necessary funds from the French Government. Collaboration had been established between this expedition and the Egyptian Government who put the author in charge of the clearing and consolidation of these pyramids so as to make their chambers accessible and safe and to collect all the inscribed fragments; the Antiquities Department supplied us with the trained foremen and workmen as well as the required equipment.

We started with the pyramid of Teti but after the first campaign in February and March 1951 work was soon interrupted by political difficulties between Egypt and France, and could not be restarted until the spring of 1956,[177] to be interrupted again only a few months later by the outbreak of hostilities consequent to the Suez Canal affair. During this much longer interruption, Jean Sainte Fare Garnot, whose health was gravely threatened, died suddenly in July 1963, just when the principle of resuming work on the pyramid of Teti had been accepted by the Egyptian Minister of Culture, Dr Saroite Okacha.

Thus it was that, in February 1965, the successor at the Sorbonne of Sainte Fare Garnot, Professor Jean Leclant, accepted the offer to continue the former's work on the 'Pyramid Texts' and, in collaboration with the Antiquities Department and myself, to resume the clearing and consolidation of Teti's burial chamber. These works produced numerous inscribed fragments and made accessible the very fine basalt royal sarcophagus, itself bearing some engraved inscriptions. In the pavement, 0·75 m. to the west of the sarcophagus and almost abutting the location of the vanished southern wall of the chamber, there was a cavity, 0·90 m. square and about as deep, that must certainly have contained the canopic chest.[178] In all, seven hundred inscribed fragments were extracted from this pyramid; they were of all sizes, many bearing only a few hieroglyphs. The inventory, the tracings and the reduced copies that were made, should now enable us to identify and link up these texts; it was established that certain of them, not included in the Maspero and Sethe publications, must belong to chapters still unknown.

*Pls. 151, 152*

At Teti's pyramid we were also able to enlarge the clearing of his funerary temple and draw up its ground plan.[179] In addition we uncovered the remains of a very fine tomb, built during the New Kingdom, just beyond the south-eastern corner of the ruined temple. It was the tomb of Akhpet, 'Truthful scribe of the king who loves him', and 'Chief of the embalmers of the master of the two lands'. Several reliefs of this official, who lived at the beginning of the XIXth Dynasty, are in a particularly fine and elegant style; in one of these he is seen wearing a wavy wig ending in a double row of small curls, and before his face, his soul is shown flying away in the form of the *ba* bird. Both the

*Pl. 153*

reliefs and his great pink anthropoid sarcophagus engraved with scenes and texts, together with its fractured lid, are still in place in the subterranean chamber.[180]

At the pyramid of Pepi I, early in 1966, we cleared the vast crater that marked the location of the burial chamber, from which the huge slabs forming the triangular vault had been partially removed and destroyed by stone robbers in the Middle Ages. During the campaign of 1966–7 we were able to complete the clearing of the descending passage and to consolidate the vestibule into which it opened where one of the huge roof-slabs and much of the eastern wall had been destroyed. Here, in the descending passage, the walls were covered with carved texts. These, starting from the vestibule and particularly in the horizontal corridor that follows it, still retain their original, and astonishingly fresh, green paint. The corridor, barred as was customary by three successive portcullises that we raised, is in a remarkable state of preservation and we can admire there, carved in the recess, the very fine details of the hieroglyphs.

*Pl. 154*

The antechamber into which the passage opened was completely blocked by fallen debris resulting from the quarrying of the walls and was in a dangerous and insecure state. This we consolidated during the campaigns of 1967–8 and 1968–9, finding some 580 fragments inscribed with 'Pyramid Texts',[181] and at the same time clearing the pyramid's northern and eastern sides. Against the latter appeared the ruins of several store-rooms of the funerary temple; these revealed the fact – which other similar examples in more heavily damaged temples had not previously shown – that they were built in two storeys. Being exceptionally well preserved, they still stood to a height of four or five metres, having been used in later times as lime kilns.

*Pl. 158*

Nearby, we found a quantity of broken, but beautiful, limestone statues representing prisoners. These statues, obviously destined for the kilns, had by good fortune been spared. The prisoners, represented kneeling and sitting on their heels, have their arms pressed against their hips and tied by three or four loops of rope passing behind the body and carefully knotted. The statues, wearing sometimes barely discernible loincloths, are only summarily treated on the lower parts of their bodies, but this is not the case for the torso above the belt, where the modelling of the muscles is quite remarkable. While their kneeling posture shows submission to the victorious king whose mercy they implore, their torsos indicate, by a slight forward

*Pl. 159*

*Pl. 160*

Pls. 161-5

leaning and by the vigorous bulging of the pectoral muscles, their vain efforts to break the bonds which hurt them – a very exceptional representation in Egyptian statuary. It was by the heads, all unfortunately more or less mutilated, that these statues – supposed to represent the different enemy races sub-jugated by the power of the pharaoh – were to be identified. Some faces, sculpted with great skill, are evidently portraits of chiefs of Asiatic and African tribes, and a study of them will possibly help in determining the ethnic environment of Egypt during the Old Kingdom.[182] To one of the Asiatic tribes it seems possible to attribute the head illustrated in Plate 165; it has long hair tied with a ribbon, a fine nose that must have been arched, high cheek-bones, and traces of a beard. Others illu-strated in Plates 163 and 164 are of a marked African type; one, wearing a striated wig, has a quietly resigned expression, strongly reminiscent of much later Buddhist art.

We do not know where these statues were situated in the royal funerary complex, but it seems likely that they were placed along the processional causeway which led from the Valley Temple to the Upper Temple and whose axis is very nearly east to west. They would have thus been distributed on each side of this axis in two groups representing respectively the conquered people of the north and of the south.

Pls. 156, 157

In the course of the campaigns of 1969–70 and 1970–1 the burial chamber, which had been terribly ravaged by the stone robbers, was cleared and consolidated. These works brought to light the beautiful pink Aswan granite chest, complete with its cover, which must have contained the canopic vases.[183] We even found a still complete packet of viscera wrapped in narrow bands, extraordinarily tight and compact, and exactly retaining the shape of the interior of the large alabaster vase that must have contained it. It lay right against the granite chest in a deep crack in the paving, made by the stone robbers perhaps in order to extract the chest, an intention that happily they did not carry out.

In clearing this chamber we gathered nearly a thousand in-scribed fragments on which, in addition to the 'Pyramid Texts' already known, some new chapters appeared.[184] The study of these fragments has already enabled Professor Leclant and Miss C. Berger, his assistant, to reconstitute on paper some large sec-tions of wall panels. More especially, on the eastern wall separating the burial chamber from its antechamber, two large inscribed fragments that had fallen down had to be replaced together with other smaller fragments in the lower courses that had disappeared under a large monolith that had slipped down about 0·80 m. due to damage caused by the quarrymen in the Middle Ages. It was thought best to raise this monolith to its original level and, in order to do this, to lighten it by breaking off all the uninscribed portion that was deeply embedded in the southern wall. After this had been done, the rest of the mono- *Pl. 157* lith, still weighing about ten tons, was raised with the help of four strong screw-jacks and restored to its original position.[185]

Important restorations are now being undertaken in this chamber where, at the bottom of its virtually untouched western wall covered with texts in beautifully formed green-painted characters, lies the lower part of the basalt sarcophagus, together with several of its fragments that can now be fitted together.

Clearing has also been carried out in the funerary temple and the double-storied store-rooms, set against the eastern face of the pyramid and separated by herring-bone walls, have now been completely excavated. Under the layers of sand and debris that covered these various store-rooms, graves, some of which go back to the XIXth Dynasty, show that the temple was already exploited as a quarry at that time; a pretty head-rest of sculpted wood engraved with the owner's name, sarcophagus masks in painted wood, and *shawabtis* (mummiform statuettes), together with numerous jars filled with grain were found.

The clearing operations, extending eastwards, reached the site of the square antechamber that preceded the offerings chamber. Its position was marked by a pink granite door jamb at its entrance and in particular by the base of its central column of the same material. This column is made from a large monolith consisting of paving element, circular base and the first 0·40 m. of the shaft which has eight unequal sides (4 wide alternating with 4 narrow). A short distance beyond, towards the north, the remains of the paving of the offerings chamber were cleared; to the east of this the remains of the five-niched sanctuary were reached, still showing *in situ* the granite paving of one of these niches, and, among the scattered blocks, a granite section from one of their framing jambs.[186] A drainage channel, already visible at the eastern extremity of the offerings chamber, passes beneath the thick wall that separates it from the sanctuary of statues and also under the latter's dug up paving. Several fragments of good-quality reliefs were unearthed, some of which showed processions of offering-bearers.

Some re-used inscribed blocks, one of which was still in place in a wall between the store-rooms near the pyramid, mention the mother of King Teti, Pepi I's grandmother.[187]

In February 1971 we started to clear the pyramid of Merenre (son and successor of Pepi I), the last of the royal pyramids with texts in which the work of restoration and research remains to be done. The entrance ramp, opened by Maspero in 1881 and afterwards sanded up again, was cleared. We found the remnants of the sanctuary situated above the entrance at the centre of the base of the north face of the pyramid; the two cornerstones of the fine limestone casing were still in place and, very near the north-western one, we found the corner block of the cornice and the top of the torus moulding.[188] A fine block bearing a relief showing a striding genie holding in one hand a long *wes* sceptre depicting the animal-god Seth, and in the other an *ankh* (the sign of life), was also found during these excavations; this genie was, of course, part of a procession of other deities walking towards the king.

In the corridor following the descending passage, now cleared of sand, the tomb robbers had by-passed the three granite portcullises lowered after the funeral to bar the way: they had pierced a tunnel through the limestone wall on the western side just before the granite facing that precedes the first of the portcullises. Thus they were able to reach its top, pass over it by taking advantage of the empty space left after its lowering and drop into the now accessible corridor by cutting through the first limestone ceiling slab beyond the third portcullis. It was by following this route that had been slightly enlarged by the quarrymen of the Middle Ages and had also been used by Maspero that we, in turn, at the end of December 1971, entered the two main rooms of the funerary chambers. They were still littered with stone fragments and fallen rubble resulting from the destruction of the walls by the medieval quarrymen.

The impression one gets in these rooms is particularly striking. The greater part of the gigantic paired blocks that form the magnificent triangular vault – like inverted 'V's decorated with white stars on a background strangely painted a sepia colour – are, in fact, literally hanging in space, held up by their own weight. This also applies to the colossal monolith, over six metres long and weighing about thirty tons, which made up the greater part of the high thick wall separating the two rooms, its lower courses having been completely removed by quarrymen. The fitting and the joining of these enormous blocks were so perfectly done that, in spite of everything, nothing had moved. The foolhardy quarrymen responsible for this destruction had stopped at the extreme limit of stability, when they became aware that the slightest additional encroachment upon what remained would be followed by very dangerous collapses. Hence, before the work of clearing of these two chambers could proceed, it was imperative that steps be taken to consolidate the most dangerous parts, and therefore to begin by properly reopening the corridor and lifting up into their slots the three granite portcullises that barred it. Only then, in February 1972, was it possible to build strong supports under the two ends of the dangerous monolith suspended between the two chambers, and start clearing around the very well-preserved basalt sarcophagus whose lid was practically intact and merely pushed back in its grooves.

About 0·60 m. from the southern end of the sarcophagus was, as in the pyramid of Pepi I, the canopic chest made of pink Aswan granite and with its bluish-black lid lying nearby. So far, no trace has been found of the canopic jars, but the numerous fragments and stone chippings that still litter the chamber may hide some surprising things. During the clearing operations we were very moved to find, at the foot of the sarcophagus and inside it, parts of newspapers discarded by Maspero: fragments of pages from *Le Temps*, *Le Figaro* and *Le Parlement*, and also from local newspapers in French, *Le Moniteur Egyptien* and *L'Union Egyptienne* – all dated March 1883.

Regarding the hieroglyphic texts, the clearing work carried out so far in this pyramid has already given us more than three hundred fragments which are the subject of study. Although always very well drawn and painted green, like those of Pepi I, the hieroglyphs of Merenre are wider and less deep and are for this reason less vigorous. The magical fear of certain wild animals is also expressed; but instead of plastering over the rear of the beast after it had been drawn and carved as was done at the pyramid of Pepi I, here it was thought sufficient, in order to render it harmless, merely to cut the animal in two by a thin painted band. Similarly, in order to eliminate any possible harmful effect resulting from representing human beings, these are only partly shown, generally the head and arms, while in the case of Pepi I human figures were, in principle, omitted.

While this work was being carried on inside the pyramid, we did some clearing to the east of the pyramid to find out what remained of the sanctuary of its temple. As was the case at Teti and at Pepi I the stela had unfortunately disappeared and only a large pink granite piece of its base was still lying there, nearly in its original place.

Immediately to the east of this point an important part of the paving of the sanctuary remains; this paving is not of alabaster as in the other royal funerary temples of the period but simply of Tura limestone. Traces can be clearly seen of the northern wall of this vast vaulted room, 10 cubits (about 5·25 m.) wide, whose eastern boundary is also visible on a paving stone, lying isolated but still *in situ*. A secondary limestone offerings table, framed on its three vertical visible sides by a small torus moulding, still stands against the site of the north wall of this room towards its western end. Immediately to the south of this table are traces of the outline of the main offerings table that must have preceded the stela. It is difficult to determine whether or not a small rectangular trough lying against the right-hand side of this offerings table and a curious basin, nearly elliptical in shape and hollowed out of the last paving stone just to the south of the axis of the hall, have a connection with the original royal funerary cult.

Near the south-eastern corner of the hall, the large quartzite sill of the door opening into the square antechamber on the south side is still in place, as is the paving of the latter with a granite slab in the centre; the missing central column must have rested on this slab, placed as in the temple of Pepi I. The sill of the door leading to the antechamber on the east is also preserved, as is part of its granite lintel carved with the name of the king.

Numerous fragments of reliefs from the offerings chamber have been collected together, all of which are simply outlined and not modelled. Their evidently unfinished state may be explained by the premature death of the king who, according to the papyrus in the Turin Museum, ruled for only four years.

97, 98 THE FUNERARY COMPLEX OF KING ZOSER

97 Gallery to the right of the descending tunnel entrance to the South Tomb; the wooden stretcher had been abandoned by those who used it to bring in the large quantity of pottery jars found there (see p. 95).

98 The top of the granite roof of the royal burial chamber beneath the Step Pyramid; towards the left edge is the three-ton granite plug, used to block the entry to the chamber below, which had been moved and slightly damaged by robbers, thus enabling them to penetrate the tomb. Note the grooves in the side of the granite plug, intended for lifting ropes. In this vault was found the foot of Zoser.

**99-101** THE FUNERARY COMPLEX OF KING ZOSER

99  A room in the underground galleries of Zoser's South Tomb; it consists of panels once decorated with blue tiles, each panel being crowned by an arch supported by *djed* pillars.

100  The frame of Zoser's dummy-door stela (illustrated in colour pl. XII), with the royal titles carved in low relief, after the blue tiles surrounding it were replaced. Note the simulated rolled mat, cleverly defined by the use of blue tiles between sculpted ties.

101  The underground chamber parallel to the one containing the dummy-door stelae, showing the indications in relief of the cross-members and hinges of the three doors (see p. 97).

102   Panel of blue tiles surmounted by *djed* pillars supporting an arch; reconstructed largely from elements found in subterranean chambers in the Step Pyramid. Cairo Museum.

103 Part of a gallery thirty-three metres beneath the Step Pyramid; discovered with its contents intact, it was full of stone vessels – most of them unfortunately crushed as a result of subsidence of the roof (see p. 100).

104 An allegorical alabaster vase for the *heb-sed* festival (see p. 133), found in one of Zoser's undergound galleries. At the base of the strap handle can be seen the double-staired platform with the thrones of Upper and Lower Egypt below two kiosks placed back to back. This group, characterizing the principal moment of the jubilee festival, is here placed over a crouched figure with upraised arms (the hieroglyphic sign for one million). The scarab on the top part of the handle symbolizes rebirth and eternity. Height 0.38 m. Cairo Museum.

105 Some of the stone vases found in the gallery seen in pl. 103 and in another gallery adjoining it (see p. 133).

106 A selection of alabaster vases from the same underground galleries, illuminated from inside to show their multi-coloured and varied veining.

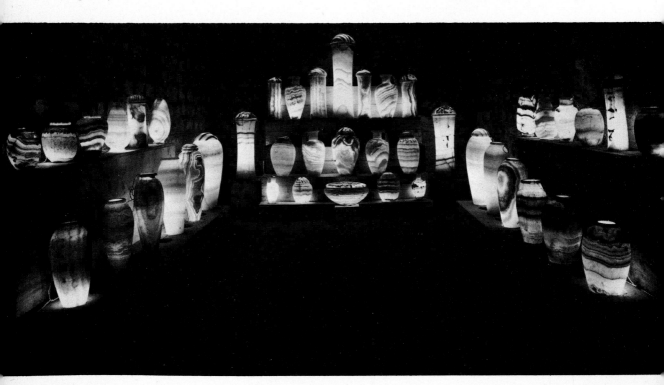

107 A double-spouted alabaster ewer.

108 A bluish-schist bowl with incised decoration imitating basketwork.

109 A blue-schist bowl imitating a metal one; note the carved simulated rivet heads.

110 View across the *heb-sed* courtyard, showing three of its pavilions and the Step Pyramid beyond.

111 General view of the rear of the buildings of the *heb-sed*; to the right is the fine curved wall that hid from view the procession as it passed from the three-columned building in the centre to the courtyard of the *sed* festival (see p. 135).

112 A curious wooden head of a woman, stuccoed and painted, found at the base of the Step Pyramid (see p. 99). XVIIIth Dynasty?; height 0·28 m. Cairo Museum.

113 THE FUNERARY COMPLEX OF THE HORUS SEKHEMKHET

The north-west corner of the foundations of Sekhem-khet's step pyramid, construction of which was interrupted by the king's premature death (see p. 137).

114

115

## 114–117 THE FUNERARY COMPLEX OF THE HORUS SEKHEMKHET

114 The north part of the first enclosure, showing the greater part of the wall preserved to a height of 3·10 m. (see p. 137).

115 A small hoard of jewellery *in situ*, found in the descending gallery of the pyramid (see p. 137).

116 The closed alabaster sarcophagus found in the burial chamber beneath the pyramid (see p. 137).

117 The shaft and the largely destroyed structure of the Sekhemkhet's south tomb (see p. 138).

118 The unfinished subterranean gallery of Sekhemkhet's south tomb and, lying across it, the crushed wooden sarcophagus of the archaic type found in it (see p. 139).

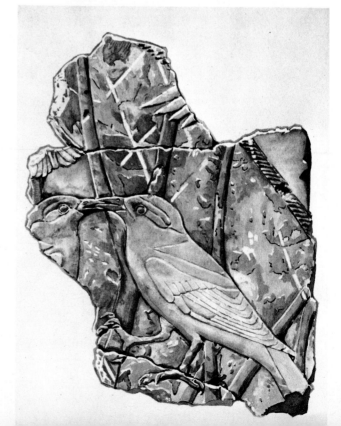

119 A relief from the temple of Userkaf's pyramid, watercolour by Mrs C. M. Firth; it shows two birds in playful conflict, against a background of branches (see p. 141).

120. Pink-granite head of a colossal statue of Userkaf, Vth Dynasty (see p. 141). Height 0.67 m. Cairo Museum.

121 Amulets and jewels found in the mummy of Wahib-re-men, a noble of the Saite period (sixth century BC), whose tomb was found intact (see p. 142). Cairo Museum.

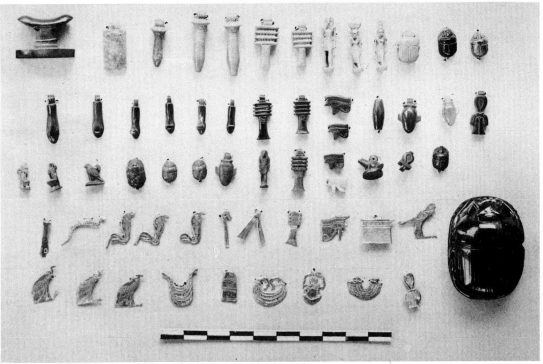

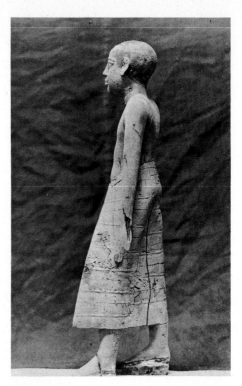

122–124   THE TOMB OF THE CHANCELLOR ISHETI

122   Head of one of the statues of Isheti, still re-taining traces of paint, notably on the wig and eyes (see p. 142). Cairo Museum.

123   One of the wooden statues found in the *serdab*. Cairo Museum.

124   The group of statues in the *serdab* of Isheti as they were found.

125–128
RELIEFS FROM THE
CAUSEWAY OF UNAS
(see p. 145)

125 Transportation of granite columns by water from Aswan for building a temple; north wall, seen *in situ*.

126 A famine scene.

127 Part of a hunting scene, showing various wild animals.

128 Goldsmiths at work; north wall, seen *in situ*.

129, 130 RELIEFS FROM THE CAUSEWAY OF UNAS (see p. 145)

129 Scenes of barter in the market-place; north wall, seen *in situ*.

130 A continuation of the scene in pl. 129, including a man exhibiting a pet ape (left).

131 THE MASTABA OF QUEEN NEBET

The queen, wife of Unas, depicted above the doorway connecting the first two rooms of the mastaba (see pp. 146–7).

132–134 THE MASTABA OF THE VIZIER MEHU

132 Entrance vestibule (Room 1), south wall: trapping birds with nets (see p. 147).

133 Room 5, south wall: a scene showing the presentation of offerings (see p. 153).

134 Room 5, east wall: two men felling an ox. Note the lyre-shaped horns and large black-spot markings.

135 Four large painted wooden statues of Akhti-hetep and one of his wife (Vth Dynasty), as found in 1940 in the *serdab* of his tomb; it contained some ten statues ranging in height from 0·90 to 1·71 m.

136–138 SCENES IN THE MASTABA OF NEFER-
HER-PTAH (see p. 154).

136   A flock of birds caught in a hexagonal net;
drawn and painted in preparation for carving.

137   A huntsman bringing in his catch and delivering
the birds to two assistants who are putting them into
cages.

138   Gardeners planting out or gathering vegetables.

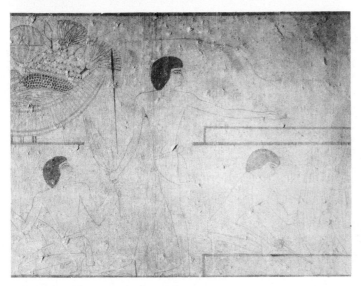

139 Vintaging scene, showing the vines supported by trellises.

140 A continuation of the vintaging scene: a group of men treading the grapes, while holding on to an overhead horizontal bar. The rhythm for the treading was provided by another man (not shown) beating time with sticks or a type of castanet.

141 A miscreant servant being beaten in the presence of an overseer on the right.

142, 143 THE MASTABA OF KHNUM-
HOTEP AND NI-ANKH-KHNUM (see
pp. 157–8)

142 The first rock-hewn chamber,
towards the south end of the west wall:
two men, either closely related or friends,
standing nose to nose and grasping
each other by the shoulder and arm.

143 The first chamber, south part of the
west wall: (reading from the lowest
register) boatmen jousting with boat-
hooks; cattle crossing a ford, preceded by
boats laden with provisions; tending of
farm animals (cf. pl. 21).

144–146 THE HYPOGEUM OF NEFER (see pp. 158–9)

144 The west wall of the single oblong chamber: this wall is almost completely occupied by the two stelae of Nefer (at the end towards the south), that of his wife Khonsu, and others of various members of his family.

145 Relief from the east wall, north section: scenes of cultivation and vintaging (cf. pl. 140).

146 The east wall, further to the south: men battling on the water; Nefer's wife with a baby and another child, and in front of them a group of dancers; preparing bread and hunting waterfowl; a herd of cattle and farmyard scenes.

147, 148   THE 'MASTABAT FARA'UN' (see p. 161)

147   The north-east corner of the strange funerary monument of King Shepseskaf, after being cleared in 1925 by G. Jéquier who can be seen leaning on one of the huge blocks of local limestone forming the first course of the structure.

148   The vaulted burial chamber from which the sarcophagus had disappeared.

149, 150 THE FUNERARY COMPLEX OF PEPI II

149 The pyramid of Pepi II and, in the foreground, the small satellite pyramid with the lower course of its casing still in place (see p. 162).

150 The burial chamber of Pepi II's pyramid after its reconstruction in 1934–5. The south and rear walls are covered with texts; the king's dark reddish-black granite sarcophagus can be seen in the foreground, with his name and titles carved in a horizontal line (barely visible in the photograph) just below the rim. Note the huge star-covered blocks forming the chamber's vaulted ceiling.

151–153 THE FUNERARY
COMPLEX OF TETI (see
pp. 178–9)

151 The pyramid of
King Teti with, in the
foreground, the ruins of his
funerary temple. On the
left, behind the small
satellite pyramid of which
only the lower part sur-
vives, the Step Pyramid and
the pyramid of Userkaf
can be seen.

152 The alabaster steps leading to the
entrance of the temple proper, of which
only the pavements and a few wall elements
and door-sills remain; in the foreground is
the block of a door-jamb carved with the
king's names and titles.

153 Relief from the tomb of the high
official Akhpet, chief of the royal embalmers,
from his tomb built in the ruins of the
entrance to the temple of Teti (probably
destroyed in the fourth century BC).

154 The remains of the triple layer of huge blocks which formed the vault of the royal burial chamber (see p. 179).

155 One of the many fragments of 'Pyramid Texts' found during the clearance of the burial chamber. Note, near the middle of the second column from the right, the hieroglyph representing a bull the front part of which only was painted green, the others being completely filled in with colour. The bull's hind-quarters are plastered, following a convention used to designate animals considered dangerous (e.g. lions, elephants); this practice was a kind of magical gesture which deprived the animal of movement and thus rendered it harmless.

156 The east wall of the royal burial chamber, covered with texts, during clearing and consolidation. The large fallen block on the right, on the south side of the roof, had to be broken and removed in order to clear the end of the chamber (see p. 180).

157 The same wall in the burial chamber after clearing and consolidation. In the foreground is the granite canopic chest for the viscera and, at the right, its lid leaning against the wall. The broken area of the text-covered wall, originally part of the huge block forming the lintel of the entrance, has fallen by about a metre.

158 The important remains of some of the
two-storeyed store-rooms built against the
east face of the pyramid. In the foreground
is the monolithic base of a granite column
with an octagonal shaft, still in its original
position; this column stood in the centre of
the square antechamber in front of the
destroyed sanctuary.

159 Two headless statues of kneeling
prisoners, two-thirds life-size; VIth Dynasty.
Obviously destined for the lime kilns, the
figures were found broken at the waist (see
pp. 179–80).

160 Back view of the statue seen on the
right in pl. 159, showing the cord used to
bind the prisoner's arms.

161–165 Five heads from similar kneeling statues of prisoners (the bodies have disappeared); these beautifully carved and expressive heads must have represented chiefs of various hostile African and Asiatic tribes (see p. 179).

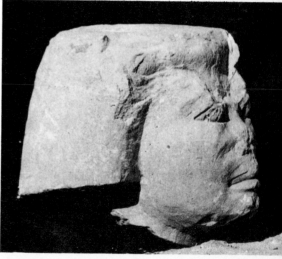

166 Some of the earthenware jars containing ibis mummies, stacked in layers (see p. 218).

167 The upper gallery with niches for baboon mummies (see p. 221). Each of the mummies – only one of them survived later desecration of the galleries by the early Christians living on the site – was placed in its small plaster sarcophagus and walled up in the niche provided.

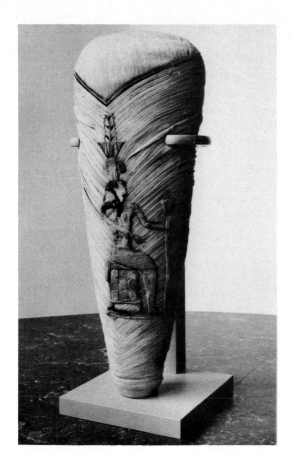

168  Ibis mummy with appliqué decoration representing the god Nefertum; height 0·48 m. British Museum, London.

169  Bronze situla with handle; its base is in the form of a lotus flower. The relief decoration is in three registers: the ape of Thoth worshipping the sun-disk in its barque; a procession of deities; the spirits of Lower Egypt. Height with handle 0·35 m. British Museum, London.

170  Typical bronze statuette of Imhotep, shown seated with a papyrus roll across his knees. Height 0·09 m. Cairo Museum.

171  Bronze figure of the god Ptah, represented in typical form wearing a close-fitting cloak with broad collar and a tight skull-cap; he holds a long *wes* sceptre Height 0·21 m. University College, London.

172 Bronze statuette of the cow-headed Isis, mother of Apis; she wears an ornate crown of plumes, horns and sun-disk above the royal uraei. The small bronze base of the figure carries a dedicatory inscription. Height 0·24 m. University College, London.

173 A bronze aegis with the head of the goddess Isis wearing a crown of uraei and flanked by two hawks. Height 0·21 m. University College, London.

174, 175 Bronze statuette of Isis nursing the infant Horus; the strips of cloth in which the statuette was wrapped when found can be seen in the photograph on the left, as well as the helmet of the Horus which was attached to one of the horns of the goddess. Height 0·27 m. University College, London.

# Recent Discoveries Made During the Search for Imhotep's Tomb

An abundance of sherds of Ptolemaic and Roman pottery, covering the western extremity of the archaic necropolis at the north of Saqqara, and in particular a wide flat expanse situated immediately to the north of a group of large IIIrd Dynasty tombs cleared by Firth, encouraged our late colleague and friend, W. B. Emery, to explore this site. He thought that the juxtaposition of the remains of these two periods, some seven hundred metres to the north of the Step Pyramid's enclosure wall, might indicate the site of the Asclepeion and of the tomb of Imhotep who had been venerated as the god of medicine during the Late Period. The tombs of the other great personages of the IIIrd Dynasty like Hesy-re, Meten, and Kha-bau-Sokar, had been discovered in this same area.

Sadly, after six campaigns (1965–70) of very fruitful excavations,[189] Emery was suddenly struck down in the midst of his work without being able to verify his hypothesis, occasionally slightly strengthened by new clues. Thus, several IIIrd Dynasty mastabas, important either by their dimensions or by various peculiarities, successively showed promise in this search. First was mastaba No. 3508, built of rough stone and encased in crude brick around which, in Ptolemaic times, the skeletons of sacrificed oxen were placed, buried at a depth of 1·30 m., and with their heads turned towards the tomb. Also, in the tomb's main pit itself, 1·25 m. below its top, an ox had been carefully enshrouded and laid upon clean sand; then, six metres lower down, Emery was astonished to find layer upon layer of over 500 slightly conical-lidded earthenware jars, each containing an ibis mummy. Some of these mummies were decorated with the image of a divinity: Thoth, the moon-god, as a baboon inside a wheeled *naos* or an ibis on a lotus flower; Isis; Hathor; Ma'at; Nefertum; and, once, Imhotep.

Nearby, against the north-eastern corner of this tomb, a mastaba (No. 3509) of the Vth Dynasty was excavated. It is stone built and belonged to a noble called Hetep-ka, who was 'Keeper of the diadem and Inspector of the king's wig-makers'.

Some fine remains of reliefs are still in place there and, again in the main pit, masses of ibis mummies were found.

*Pl. 166*

A few metres to the east of the IIIrd Dynasty tomb No. 3508, a second tomb of the same period (No. 3510) was uncovered and, through its southern pit, at a depth of about ten metres, a vast labyrinth of underground galleries branching off from a central curved gallery, was discovered. Several of these, 4·50 m. high and 2·50 m. wide, were completely filled with ibis mummies still intact in their pots. It was only later – in the following season – that the entrance to these galleries was found. This was reached by a staircase next to a small Ptolemaic temple dedicated to the god Thoth, according to the ostraca – limestone flakes or pottery sherds used for writing on, in place of papyrus – that were found there (19 in demotic, 2 in Greek and 2 bilingual). Most of the demotic texts are complaints or supplications to Thoth, or decisions announced by his oracles. Isis is the only other divinity mentioned, in seven of these documents.

Could these be the galleries that the traveller Paul Lucas said that he had reached in 1716 and followed for a distance of four kilometres? Seen again later by Pococke and Vivant Denon, they appear in the plates illustrating the *Description de l'Egypte* entitled 'The tombs of the bird mummies', and were, at that time, one of the principal monuments of Saqqara. It was logical to suppose that the entrance found was probably not the only one, nor even the main one to these extremely extensive galleries with their ibis mummies piled in their tens of thousands.

*Pl. 168*

On many of the mummies examined, the most frequent appliqué decorations were those of Thoth, Isis and Nefertum, together with their emblems and more especially those of the latter,[190] also present are Hathor, Ma'at, the cynocephalic baboon, and even Imhotep.

Sixty metres to the east of the furthermost point reached in these tunnels a big tomb of the IIIrd Dynasty (No. 3517) was found. Measuring 56 m. × 25 m., it is the largest of those discovered until now in this northern cemetery. It had been destroyed and levelled to a height of one metre above its base, doubtless during Ptolemaic times, when sacrificed oxen had been buried to the east of each of its two shafts; however, except for a few fragments of good-quality stone vessels, typical of the IIIrd Dynasty, nothing gives us any clue as to the person who had been buried there.

Further clearing was then carried out, 250 metres to the north, at a site overlooking the path that leads from the village of Abusir to the Serapeum, and where aerial photographs had revealed the presence of a rectangular enclosure. Inside this enclosure the platform of a systematically destroyed temple was uncovered, and numerous small statues and other bronze objects were found. Carefully dressed or stuccoed limestone blocks, evidently belonging to this temple and bearing demotic ink graffiti invoking 'Isis, mother of Apis', lead one to suppose that this is her temple; especially as, in addition, prayers to this goddess appear on small votive stelae, offerings tables, and on some two hundred ostraca (written mostly in demotic) found nearby. In addition, numerous papyri found during the excavations, span the period between the seventh and third centuries BC. They are now being studied, and will doubtless give much useful information: of these texts, 306 are in demotic, 51 in Aramaic script, 4 in late hieratic, and 2 (of which one would appear not to be in Greek) in Greek uncials of the fourth century BC.

As the site thereabouts was much destroyed, Emery extended his excavations towards the south where mounds of sand and debris indicated a vast structure (sectors 3, 4 and 5 on his maps). Another platform, against which ended a ramp coming from the west, was uncovered. This platform was covered by the tumbled remains of houses of the Christian era and, hidden in one of the walls, a small hoard of coins was discovered: eleven fourth-century AD Roman gold solidi of the emperors Constantius II, Julian II, Valentinian I, Valens, Theodosius I and Arcadius.

The discovery of pottery torch-handles among the rubbish of sector 4 indicated that an entrance to underground passages could not be far away, and that these could have been consecrated to the cows, mothers of the Apis bulls, because of the previously mentioned inscriptions addressed to Isis, mother of Apis. At the same time quantities of bovine bones, sometimes still covered with wrappings, found in some parts of this debris, were clearly the result of the plundering of their tombs. But the entrance was not found; instead another IIIrd Dynasty tomb appeared, deeply buried about twenty metres to the west of the angle formed by the ramp and the wall of the platform of sector 3, at the base of which other deposits of statuettes and high-quality bronze religious objects were found. Perhaps those had *Pls. 169, 173* formed part of a superabundance of gifts to the temple, which had been buried within the sacred enclosure by the priests who were prevented from destroying them because of their sacred nature. Similar caches to the east of the same wall yielded other remarkable objects.[191]

Also found during this vast clearing was a small, crude brick, vaulted building containing three rooms with a single common entrance towards the east. In its main room was a quantity of cattle bones and skulls, some of which were covered with painted gesso. After successive layers of such animal remains had been removed, a curious, intact, simulated ox or cow mummy appeared: the body, too small for the head, was made up of planks of wood, carefully shaped and covered with painted gesso with the characteristic Apis markings.[192] Painted cattle skulls found among these bones above this 'false' mummy must have belonged to others destroyed by plunderers.

Still not having found in sector 4 the entrance to the underground passages, Emery decided to uncover systematically, layer by layer, the platform of the adjacent sector 3. This revealed, in the upper level, a Christian establishment, probably a monastery with a church in whose foundations of crude bricks had been incorporated palm-shaped capitals copying those of the Vth Dynasty, and various other architectural elements with engraved cartouches of Nectanebo II; on one of these, a large lintel, the king presents offerings to Apis shown as a man with the head of a bull.[193] It is therefore to Nectanebo II, the last native pharaoh, that we owe this temple which seems to have been dedicated to Isis, mother of Apis. As to the destruction of the temple, the Christian remains that were brought to light, as well as the hoard of eleven Roman gold solidi, indicate that it must have taken place towards the end of the fourth century consequent upon the Edict of Theodosius.

It was only after the removal of these buildings that the ruins of buildings contemporary with Nectanebo II appeared. On each side of the principal sanctuary that had been re-used unchanged by the Christians, three others have left traces: one to the north and two to the south. All had been built at right-angles to the escarpment and were preceded by a stair-ramp. Various caches of votive objects were discovered there; the most important, in a pit hidden under the passage of the north sanctuary, included numerous bronze statuettes, mostly of Osiris, Isis and Harpocrates, some of Apis and Ptah and one of Imhotep. Many of these statuettes had been carefully wrapped before being placed inside three wooden *naos*, and some were still covered with linen.

After having emptied this pit, the examination of its lining showed that it was made up of ten re-used stelae: five with hieroglyphic texts, four with Carian texts and one uninscribed.

*Pls. 170–2*

*Pls. 174, 175*

On the better of the Carian stelae, a man and a woman are shown face to face, both wearing Carian dress.[194] These strange stelae had presumably been taken from nearby graves when Nectanebo built his temple.

Behind the southernmost sanctuary, after removing a filling of stone chippings from between two dry-stone walls built at right-angles to the escarpment, there appeared against the latter an entrance built of dressed stone and crowned by a cavetto cornice. This entrance, walled up with dressed stones, had been broken down by plunderers; it opened on to a vestibule giving access to galleries containing the burials of baboons. The soft limestone walls of these galleries are lined with fine limestone masonry still perfectly preserved in many places. On each side at about one metre from the ground are niches in which the mummies of the baboons were deposited. The main galleries are on two different levels linked to each other by a stairway. As they were very dangerous at several points, they could be completely cleared only after the necessary consolidation works had been carried out.

*Pl. 167*

In the floor at the south-eastern corner of the vestibule, a shaft gives access to another subterranean complex of baboon burials and it was there that the only two burials untouched during later Christian occupation of the site were found. 'The animal,' wrote Emery about one of them, 'was mummified and wrapped in the usual manner. It was then placed upright in a wooden chest which was then filled, in some cases with gypsum plaster, and in others with cement. The chests with their solidified contents were placed in the niches which were sealed with a stone blocking on which a demotic inscription was written in ink ...'[195] These texts give the date of the baboon's burial, generally his name and a short prayer for his eternal happiness. Sometimes it was also stated where the animal came from and when he had been installed in the temple of Ptah.

At the bottom of the stairs leading to the lower gallery two life-size baboon statues were found.[196] But the most important finds came from one of these lower galleries, dubbed 'C' by Emery, where further limestone false-door stelae engraved with short Carian texts were found among the rubble.[197] These stelae, taken from a nearby cemetery (like those of the pit-lining already mentioned), had been re-used in the masonry; the proof was provided by another Carian stela re-used in the casing of the upper gallery. It is also to be noted that, among the graffiti on the gallery walls, written generally by visitors, only one occurs in Carian whereas there are about a hundred in demotic and some in hieroglyphs.

Some very peculiar objects were also found in the rubble of the upper gallery. They were plaster casts of various parts of the human body: complete heads, upper halves of faces, hair, torsos, hands, legs and feet, etc. There is no doubt that these were medical votive offerings placed there by sick pilgrims,[198] either to indicate to the god the nature of their illness or the part of the body to be cured, or as an expression of gratitude for a cure obtained.

The complete clearing of these baboon galleries made it possible to establish two important facts. The first was that, in the lower gallery soon after the stairs, a large breach between two adjoining niches gave access to another gallery filled from top to bottom with ibis mummies in intact pottery jars; thousands of these mummies blocked the way, and it was impossible to enter very far, but it was thus seen that a connection existed between the ibis galleries and those of the baboons, even though their respective entrances were over two hundred metres apart. The second important point was that the main upper gallery runs westwards directly to the tomb of Kha-bau-Sokar (No. 3073), very near to the centre of the IIIrd Dynasty cemetery; but, long before reaching it, at a distance of 32 m. from the entrance, the gallery cuts through an earlier pit that reaches, lower down, to a funerary chamber still containing an empty archaic sarcophagus. On the surface, this pit was found to belong to a large mastaba (52 × 19 m.) of the IIIrd Dynasty with a double chapel (No. 3518) and whose second pit, further north, is not joined to the baboon gallery; this second pit, which had been plundered, contains an important quantity of broken stone vessels of good quality and, in the store-rooms of the mastaba's superstructure, behind the north chapel, there are still stores of jars of the period among which a large clay stopper bears the seal impression of the Horus Neterikhet (Zoser).[199] Emery also noted that this mastaba was oriented in exactly the same way as the Step Pyramid, while nearly all the other tombs of that period were oriented quite differently. Finally, the clearing of the area in front of the principal entrance (south) produced a whole hoard of anatomic plaster replicas, made for presentation like those previously discovered among the rubble of the baboon gallery.

The completion of the excavations in sector 3 with the location of the entrance to the baboon galleries, produced a further important group of written documents: hieroglyphic inscriptions on architectural fragments of Old Kingdom mastabas, funerary stelae from the Ramesside period to the Roman and, especially, twenty-seven demotic ostraca, as well as two in Greek and one in Coptic, that are extremely valuable for the interpretation of the site. Among those written in demotic, is a contract of Year 9 of Darius I (513 BC), 'apparently of self-dedication, a complaint to Isis, and a dream text', writes Professor H. S. Smith in his report. Among some papyri was a nearly complete marriage document in demotic dated Year 11 of Darius (most probably Darius I), and also two short fragments in Greek and one in Aramaic.

During the winter of 1970–1, in spite of the necessity of undertaking important and elaborate shoring work in the vast underground galleries of the new Serapeum (probably of the mothers of the Apis bulls), whose entrance Emery finally discovered about fifty metres to the north of the baboon galleries, the excavations continued. They led to the discovery of yet more galleries: some, situated south of those of the baboons, were reserved for thousands of mummies of hawks and other birds of prey, sometimes quite large ones. Other galleries reached by a long and wide stairway, are situated more than two hundred metres away towards the north, on the other side of the spur formed by the cliff at that point. They also contain a considerable quantity of ibis mummies and seem to be greater and even more extensive than those of the first group discovered five years ago.

One is astounded by the enormous quantity of these various mummified birds, whose number must easily exceed a million, and by the extent of the extraordinary network of galleries excavated for their burial, the boundaries of which have still not been reached. It is advisable therefore, to explore systematically these galleries in all their ramifications in order to draw up a complete plan and establish their connections with the remains of the various exterior monuments of the Late Period as well as of the IIIrd Dynasty. It was on this work that Emery was actively engaged when he suffered a stroke on the site of the excavations, and it is highly desirable that his work, that has already produced so much, should be continued and completed by his colleagues and fellow scholars.

Once the plan of the underground galleries and of the architectural remains on the surface has been established, the cult objects collected, and especially once the very numerous written documents mentioned have been studied, they will throw a new light upon the interpretation of these strange animal cults that became so widespread in the last period of ancient Egyptian civilization, and that were only definitively abolished several centuries after the Roman conquest by the victory of Christianity over paganism. From this point of view alone, would it not be as worthy an achievement as the discovery of Imhotep's tomb itself?

# Epilogue

The very numerous and important discoveries described in this volume span, as we have seen, over 4,000 years of history, from the time of the union of Upper with Lower Egypt, brought about by Menes *c.* 3000 BC, to the destruction of the Coptic monastery of St Jeremiah by the Arabs *c.* AD 960. How many archaeological sites are there – not only in Egypt but in the whole world – that have produced such a quantity of monuments, works of art, texts, documents written or otherwise, vases and objects of all sorts, spanning such a long historical period, as has the Saqqara necropolis? Furthermore, some one hundred and twenty-five years of exploration and excavation since the first discovery of the Serapeum are far from having exhausted all that lies here, covered and perhaps providentially preserved by the eternal sands.

The site of Saqqara thus appears as the principal highlight of the civilization of ancient Egypt preceding, as it does, that of Thebes by a thousand years. It undoubtedly deserves much greater attention than that given to it so parsimoniously by most of the organized tours to Egypt. Would it not be very much worthwhile if visitors could give at least a whole day to its discovery, instead of only one or two hours, as is so often the case?

In Upper Egypt it is essentially the art of the New Kingdom that flourishes and is of the greatest interest, but with its own very different character. There is, however, nothing to compare with Old Kingdom survivals, such as the magnificent IIIrd Dynasty monuments built by the masterly Imhotep, or with the precious 'Pyramid Texts' of the Vth and VIth Dynasties and the well-known mastabas of nobles and high officials of that period – all of which are the pride of Saqqara.

If this volume is in any way instrumental in producing a better organization for visiting this site, venerable amongst all others and yet so near to Cairo, its production will not have been in vain; this is my most ardent desire.

# Notes to the Text

*For abbreviations of journals etc. cited, see Bibliography*

### INTRODUCTION

1 To reach the Saqqara necropolis from Memphis, the use of canals must have been necessary.
2 Skins of sacred animals, symbolizing rebirth, worn by the Bacchantes.
3 Rods topped with pine-cones and garlanded with ivy, carried by Dionysos and by Bacchantes.
4 Stibadeia were small sanctuaries in the cult of Dionysos; one example, discovered at Thebes, is roughly contemporary with the semi-circle of poets and philosophers at Saqqara, and has clear parallels with it. At Thasos, however, it was Dionysos himself who presided, not Homer as at Saqqara, but Dionysos had come to be regarded in Greece as the patron of literary activities, sharing this role with Apollo Musagetes (leader of the Muses).
5 The engineer Linant de Bellefonds was then Director-General of Public Works in Egypt; Dr Clot, founder of the School of Medicine in Cairo, was responsible for the Health Department. During his remarkable reign, Mohammed Ali had in effect entrusted important functions to several Frenchmen who had come to Egypt, such as Colonel Sève, instructor and later commander-in-chief of the army, known as Soliman Pasha; the engineer Charles Lambert, who was head of the Ecole Polytechnique de Boulaq and worked with Linant de Bellefonds on the construction of the Nile Delta barrage.

### CHAPTER I

6 Auguste Mariette, *Le Sérapéum de Memphis* (published posthumously by G. Maspero), p. 4.
7 Ibid., pp. 5–6.
8 Strabo, *Geography*, Book XVII, dealing with Egypt and North Africa.
9 Mariette, op. cit., p. 7.
10 See J.-Ph. Lauer and Ch. Picard, *Les statues ptolémaïques du Sarapiéion de Memphis*, especially pp. 108–18.
11 Mariette, op. cit., pp. 17–18.
12 See Lauer and Picard, op. cit., pp. 10–19.
13 Only one of the black marks is still visible on the end of the spine of the bull exhibited in the Louvre.

14 See Mariette, *Notice des principaux monuments exposés au Musée d'Antiquités égyptiennes de S. A. le Vice-roi à Boulaq*, (1st ed., 1864) p. 61, (6th ed., 1878) p. 94, No. 26; also Arthur Rhoné, *L'Egypte à petites journées* (new ed., 1910), p. 224.
15 See 'Notice biographique d'Auguste Mariette', in *Bibl. égyptol.*, XVIII (1904), p. LIII.
16 H. Brugsch, *Mein Leben und mein Wandern*, pp. 165–6.
17 The name by which the historian Manetho (third century BC) designated Horemheb, last king of the XVIIIth Dynasty.

### CHAPTER II

18 Mariette, 'Notice sur l'état actuel et sur les résultats, jusqu'à ce jour, des travaux entrepris pour la conservation des antiquités égyptiennes en Egypte', in *CRAIB*, III (1862), pp. 153 ff.
19 'Notice biographique d'Auguste Mariette', op. cit., p. LXXXVIII.
20 Mariette, 'Sur les tombes de l'Ancien Empire que l'on trouve à Saqqarah', in *RA*, 19 (1869), pp. 7–8.
21 G. Devéria, 'Théodule Devéria, Notice biographique', pp. XIV–XVI, *Bibl. égyptol.*, IV.
22 *Notice des princip. monum. exposés au Musée d'Antiquités égyptiennes à Boulaq*, No. 492.
23 P. Montet, *Scènes de la vie privée dans les tombeaux égyptiens de l'Ancien Empire*, p. 284.
24 Ibid., pp. 295–7 and fig. 40.
25 Ibid., p. 304.
26 Ibid., pp. 311–12 and fig. 41.
27 Ibid., p. 322.
28 J. Vandier, *Manuel d'Archéologie*, V, p. 109.
29 Ibid., p. 65.
30 P. Montet, op. cit., pp. 223–4.
31 Ibid., pp. 334–46.
32 See, for example, K. Lange and M. Hirmer, *Egypt: Architecture, Sculpture, Painting*, pls. 61, 64, 65, or E. Drioton and A. Vigneau, *Le Musée du Caire* (Encyclopédie photographique de l'Art), Paris 1949, pls. 23–5.
33 See *RA*, 11 (1860), p. 23.
34 See, for example, Drioton and Vigneau, op. cit., fig. 4.
35 J. E. Quibell, *Excavations at Saqqara (1911–1912)*. The tomb of Hesy.

### CHAPTER III

36 J. de Morgan, *Fouilles à Dahchour, mars-juin 1894, and 1894–1895*, 2 vols., Vienna 1895, 1903.

37 Montet, *Scènes de la vie privée*, pp. 88, 89.
38 Ibid., p. 286.
39 Montet, op. cit., pp. 368–71.
40 Vandier, op. cit., IV, p. 514.
41 Ibid., p. 522.
42 Ibid., p. 518.
43 H. Hickmann, 'La danse aux miroirs', *BIE*, XXXVII, 1 (1956), pp. 151–90.
44 See on this subject, Montet, op. cit., pp, 113–14. In a hunting scene of Ptah-hotep (here Plate 57) two hyenas appear, in fact, to be ready for action.
45 On these masts and their working, see Vandier, *Manuel d'Archéologie*, V, pp. 796–7.
46 On the roles of these boatswains, see Vandier, op. cit., pp. 718–21; and Ch. Boreux, *Etudes de nautique égyptienne*, pp. 404–11.
47 Vandier, op. cit., IV, p. 493.
48 Montet, op. cit., pp. 365–8.
49 L. Keimer, in *Revue de l'Egypte ancienne*, I (1927), pp. 182 ff.; II (1929), pp. 210–15, and III (1930), pp. 36–41.
50 V. Loret, *Fouilles dans la nécropole memphite (1897–1899). Communication faite à l'Institut Egyptien dans la séance du 5 mai 1899*, Cairo 1899; also J. Capart, *Une rue de tombeaux à Saqqarah*, 2 vols., Brussels 1907.
51 N. de G. Davies, *The Mastaba of Ptahhetep and Akhethetep at Saqqarah*, 2 vols., London 1900, 1901.
52 Montet, op. cit., p. 371, and Vandier, op. cit., p. 518.
53 Montet, op cit., pp. 78–80, and Vandier, op. cit., IV, pp. 473–9.
54 Barsanti and Maspero, 'Fouilles autour de la pyramide d'Ounas', *ASAE*, I–III, V.
55 Quibell, *Excavations at Saqqara (1905–1906)*, Cairo 1907.
56 Quibell, *Excavations at Saqqara (1906–1907)*, Cairo 1908.
57 Quibell, ibid.; also *Excavations at Saqqara (1907–1908)* and *(1908–1910)*, and *The Monastery of Apa Jeremias*, p. 7, and pls. VIII, XIII.
58 Quibell, *Excavations at Saqqara (1912–1914)*, *Archaic Mastabas*.
59 Quibell, *Excavations at Saqqara (1911–1912)*. *The tomb of Hesy*.
60 See C. M. Firth in *ASAE*, XXXI, pp. 45–8 and plate.
61 See Drioton-Vigneau, op. cit., fig. 41.
62 C. M. Firth and B. Gunn, *Excavations at Saqqara. Teti Pyramid Cemeteries*, 2 vols., Cairo 1926.
63 Firth, 'Preliminary report on the excavations at Saqqara (1925–1926)', *ASAE*, XXVI, p. 101, and pl. IV (A), v.
64 R. Macramallah, *Fouilles à Saqqarah. Le mastaba de Idout*, Cairo 1935.
65 Z. Y. Saad, 'Preliminary report on the Excavations of the Dept. of Antiquities at Saqqara (1942–43)', *ASAE*, XLIII, pp. 449–57, and pls. XXXIII–XLVI; also Drioton, *Description sommaire des chapelles funéraires de la VIème dynastie récemment découvertes derrière le mastaba de Mérérouka à Sakkarah*, pp. 487–513, and pl. XLVII.

CHAPTER IV

66 W. B. Emery, *The Tomb of Hemaka*, Cairo 1938; *Excavations at Saqqara, 1937–1938*, and *Hor Aha*, Cairo, 1939.
67 Emery, *Great Tombs of the First Dynasty*, I, Cairo 1949.
68 Emery, *Great Tombs of the First Dynasty*, II & III, London 1954, 1958.
69 Emery, *Hor Aha*, pp. 1–7.
70 Emery, *Great Tombs*, II, pp. 1–4, and Lauer, *Histoire monumentale des pyramides d'Egypte*, I, pp. 33–5.
71 Lauer, 'Evolution de la tombe royale égyptienne jusqu'à la Pyramide à degrés', *MDAIK*, 15, pp. 148–65.
72 Emery, *Great Tombs*, II, pp. 1–4, 5–127, and pls. I–XXXVII.
73 Ibid., p. 142.
74 Ibid., pls. XXVI–XXXVII.
75 Emery, *Great Tombs*, I, pp. 20–57 and pls. 4–10.
76 Emery, *The Tomb of Hemaka*, pls. 11–23.
77 Emery, *Great Tombs*, III, pls. 2, 24, 25, 27.

CHAPTER V

78 Firth and Quibell, *The Step Pyramid*, I, pp. 77–85.
79 See Firth, 'Two mastaba chapels of the IIIrd Dynasty at Sakkara', in *ASAE*, XXIV, pp. 122–7 and 3 plates.
80 Firth, ibid., pls. 1, 2, and 'Excavations of the Dept. of Antiquities at the Step Pyramid, Saqqara (1924–1925)', in *ASAE*, XXV, pp. 149–59 and 5 plates. See also Lauer, *La Pyramide à degrés. L'architecture*, II, pls. LVI, LIX, LXIII.
81 Firth, 'Preliminary report on the excavations at Saqqara (1925–1926)', *ASAE*, XXVI, pp. 97–101 and 5 plates; also Lauer, op. cit., pls. XXXVIII–XLVIII.
82 B. Gunn, 'Inscriptions from the Step Pyramid site', *ASAE*, XXVI, pp. 177–96 and plate.
83 Lauer, 'Étude sur quelques monuments de la IIIème dynastie', *ASAE*, XXVII, pp. 112–21 and pls. I, II.
84 Lauer, *La Pyramide à degrés. L'architecture*, I, pp. 154–77, and II, pls. LXXIII, LXXXI.
85 Firth in *ASAE*, XXVII, pp. 105–11 and 3 plates.
86 Lauer, *La Pyramide à degrés. L'architecture*, I, pp. 101 ff., and II, pl. XXXI.
87 See Lauer and Derry, 'Découverte à Saqqarah d'une partie de la momie du roi Zoser', in *ASAE*, XXXV, pp. 25–7 and plate.
88 Firth, in *ASAE*, XXVIII, pp. 81–8 and 3 plates.
89 Lauer in *ASAE*, XXXVIII, pp. 551–65 and pls. C, CI.
90 Lauer, *Histoire monumentale des pyramides d'Egypte*, I, *Les pyramides à degrés (IIIème dynastie)*, pp. 131–42.

91 Lauer, V. Laurent Täckholm and E. Äberg, 'Les plantes découvertes dans les souterrains de l'enceinte du roi Zoser', in *BIE*, XXXII, pp. 121–57 and plates.

92 Firth in *ASAE*, XXVIII, pp. 82–3.

93 Lauer, in *ASAE*, XXX, pp. 137–40 and pl. I.

94 Lauer, in *ASAE*, XXXIX, p. 450, and pl. LXX; also *Drioton and Vigneau*, op. cit., p. 24 and pl. 89.

95 Lauer, in *ASAE*, XXX, pp. 129–36 and pl. I; *ASAE*, XXXI, pp. 65–9 and pls. I, II.

96 *ASAE*, XXXIII, pp. 146–52 and plate.

97 Lauer, 'Fouilles du Service des Antiquités à Saqqarah (Secteur Nord), nov. 1932–mai 1933', *ASAE*, XXXIII, pp. 155–66 and pls. I, II.

98 Lauer, 'Fouilles . . . à Saqqarah, nov. 1933–mai 1934', *ASAE*, XXXIV, pp. 54–62 and pls. I, II; also in *ASAE*, XXXV, pp. 66–75, and pls. I, II; *ASAE*, XXXVI, pp. 20–8 and pls. I, II.

99 Lauer, *La Pyramide à degrés*, III, *Compléments*. Cairo 1939.

100 P. Lacau and J.-Ph. Lauer, *La Pyramide à degrés*, IV, *Inscriptions gravées sur les vases*, 2 vols., Cairo 1959, 1961.

101 Lacau and Lauer, *La Pyramide à degrés*, V, *Inscriptions à l'encre sur les vases*, Cairo 1965.

102 Lauer, in *ASAE*, XXXVII, pp. 96–100 and pls. I, II.

103 Lauer, in *ASAE*, XXXIX, pp. 469–72 and pls. LXXII, LXXIII.

104 Lauer, 'Restaurations et "anastylose" dans les Monuments du roi Zoser à Saqqarah (1927–1947)', in *ASAE*, XLVIII, pp. 351–66 and pls. I–III.

105 Lauer, in *ASAE*, LIV, pp. 101–10 and pls. I–III.

106 Lauer, 'Travaux de restitution et d'anastylose en cours dans les Monuments du roi Zoser à Saqqarah', in *CRAIB*, 1963, pp. 301–12; also in *CRAIB*, 1966, pp. 453–6.

107 *CRAIB*, 1967, pp. 494–6, and *CRAIB*, 1969, pp. 460–3.

108 *CRAIB*, 1970, pp. 484–8.

109 *CRAIB*, 1973, p. 325 and pl. II (*b*).

CHAPTER VI

110 Zakaria Goneim, *Horus Sekhem-khet. The unfinished step pyramid at Saqqara*, I, Cairo 1957.

111 Z. Goneim, op. cit., pp. 13–14, and pls. XXXI–XXXIV.

112 Lauer, 'L'apport historique des récentes découvertes du Service des Antiquités de l'Egypte dans la nécropole memphite', *CRAIB*, pp. 372–3.

113 Z. Goneim, op. cit., pl. LX.

114 Lauer, 'Travaux d'anastylose et nouvelles recherches sur les pyramides et leurs complexes à Saqqarah, de 1964 à 1966', *CRAIB*, 1966, pp. 456–8.

115 Lauer, 'Recherche et découverte du tombeau Sud de l'Horus Sekhem-khet dans son complexe funéraire à Saqqarah', *RE*, 20, pp 97–107 and pls. 5, 6; also in *CRAIB*, 1967, pp. 496–508.

CHAPTER VII

116 Lauer, in *CRAIB*, 1969, p. 463.

117 Firth, in *ASAE*, XXIX, pp. 64–70, and pls. I, II.

118 Drioton and Lauer, 'Les tombes jumelées de Neferibrê-sa-Neith et de Ouahibrê-men', in *ASAE*, LI, pp. 469, 478–9 and pl. I.

119 Ibid., pp. 469–90 and pls. I–XVI.

120 Zaki Y. Saad, in *ASAE*, XLI, pp. 391–3 and pls. XXVIII–XXX; also Drioton in *ASAE*, LII, pp. 105–28, and Lauer, ibid., pp. 133–6 and pls. I, II.

121 Lauer, 'Le temple haut de la pyramide du roi Ouserkaf à Saqqarah', *ASAE*, LIII, pp. 119–33 and pls. I–IV.

122 Lauer, 'Découverte du serdab du chancelier Icheti à Saqqarah', in *RE*, VII, pp. 15–18 and pls. I, II; also Drioton and Lauer, 'Un groupe de tombes à Saqqarah: Icheti, Nefer-khouou-Ptah, Sebek-em-khent et Ankhi', *ASAE*, LV, pp. 207–51 and pls. I–XXV.

123 A. Barsanti, 'Le mastaba de Samnofir', *ASAE*, I, pp. 150–60. This mastaba, now covered with sand, is no longer accessible.

124 Barsanti and Maspero, 'Les tombeaux de Psammétique et de Setariban', in *ASAE*, I, pp. 161–88.

125 Ibid., pp. 262–81.

126 Ibid., pp. 230–61.

127 Ibid., pp. 234–5.

128 *ASAE*, II, p. 235.

129 A plan of this extraordinarily intensive subterranean tomb has been published by Lauer, *La Pyramide à degrés. L'architecture*, I, p. 4, fig. 2, and *Hist. monum. des pyr. d'Egypte*, I, pl. 6a.

130 Maspero, 'Note sur les objets recueillis sous la pyramide d'Ounas', in *ASAE*, III, pp. 185–90.

131 Lauer, *Hist. monum.*, I, pp. 56–9.

132 Firth in *ASAE*, XXX, pp. 185–9 and plate.

133 Lauer in *ASAE*, XXXVII, pp. 111–13 and plate.

134 Selim Hassan, in *ASAE*, XXXVIII, pp. 503–21 and pls. XCIV–XCVII.

135 Ibid., pp. 512–19 and pl. XCVII (B).

136 Ibid., pp. 519–21 and pls. XCIV–XCVII (A).

137 See on this subject the interesting article by G. Goyon, 'Les navires de transport de la chaussée monumentale d'Ounas', in *BIFAO*, LXIX (1970), pp. 11–41 and pls. I–VII.

138 Selim Hassan, op. cit., pl. XCV.

139 Montet, *Scènes de la vie privée*, pp. 275–88.

140 Drioton, in *BIE* (1943), pp. 45–54 and fig. 3; also S. Schott, 'Aufnahmen von Hungersnotrelief aus dem Aufweg der Unaspyramide', in *RE*, 17 (1965).

141 Selim Hassan, op. cit., p. 521.

142 *ASAE*, XLI, pp. 382–91 and pls. XXVI, XXVII.

143 Zaki Y. Saad, 'A preliminary report on the excavations at Saqqara, 1939-1940', *ASAE*, XL, pp. 683–5.

144 Ibid., pp. 683–4 and pls. LXXVIII, LXXIX.

145 Ibid., pp. 685–6.

146 Ibid., pp. 686–7.

147 Ibid., pp. 687–92 and pls. LXXX, LXXXI.

148 Ibid., pp. 690–2.

149 Abdel Salam M. Hussein, 'Fouilles sur la chaussée d'Ounas (1941-1943)', *ASAE*, XLIII, pp. 439–42 and pls. XXVIII–XXXII.

150 Abd El-Hamid Zayed, 'Le Tombeau d'Akhti-hotep à Saqqara', *ASAE*, LV, I, pp. 127–37 and pls. I–XVII.

151 Drioton, in *BIE*, XXVI, pp. 77–90; also G. Brunton in *ASAE*, XLVII, pp. 125–33 and pls. XV, XVI.

152 See in Prisse d'Avennes, *Histoire de l'Art Egyptien*; this drawing of the sarcophagus is reproduced by J. Capart, *L'Art Egyptien*, I, *L'Architecture* (1922), pl. 23. The fragments of the sarcophagus discovered in the Mastabat Fara'un also have similar torus corners (cf. p. 161).

153 *BIE*, XXVI, p. 88 and fig. 6.

154 Ibid., p. 88, fig. 7.

155 Montet, *Scènes de la vie privée*, pp. 75–7 and pl. VII (1), in which similar scenes shown in the mastaba of Ti are described and discussed.

156 This tomb was published by Ahmed Musa and H. Altenmüller, *The Tomb of Nefer at Sakkara*, in *Archäologische Veröffentlichungen des Deutschen Archäologischen Instituts, Abteilung Kairo*, 5, 1971.

CHAPTER VIII

157 G. Jéquier, *Le Mastabat Faraoun*, pp. 9–11.

158 Ibid., pp. 21, 31, 32.

159 Jéquier, *Le Monument funéraire de Pepi II*, I–III.

160 Jéquier, *La pyramide d'Oudjebten*.

161 Jéquier, *Les pyramides des reines Neit et Apouit*.

162 L. Borchardt, *Das Grabdenkmal des Königs Ne-user-Rê*, Leipzig 1907; *Das Grabdenkmal des Königs Nefer-ir-ka-Rê*, Leipzig 1909; *Das Grab-denkmal des Königs Sahu-Rê*, 2 vols., Leipzig 1910, 1913.

163 Jéquier, *La pyramide d'Oudjebten*, pls. III, VI–XII; also *Les pyramides des reines Neit et Apouit*, pls. VII–XXXII, XXXVIII, XXXIX.

164 Jéquier, *La pyramide d'Aba*, pls. III–XVI.

165 Jéquier, *Tombeaux de particuliers contemporains de Pépi II*.

166 Jéquier, *Douze ans de fouilles dans la nécropole memphite, 1924-1936*, p. 109, fig. 30.

167 Ibid., p. 110.

168 Ibid., p. 112, fig. 31.

169 Ibid., p. 118, fig. 32.

170 Jéquier, ibid., p. 130, fig. 37; also 'A propos d'une statue de la VIème dynastie', *Mémoires de l'IFAO*, LXVI (Mélanges Maspero, vol. I), pp. 105–12.

171 J. de Morgan, *Carte de la nécropole memphite*, pl. VI.

172 Jéquier, *Deux pyramides du Moyen Empire*, p. 8, fig. 7.

173 Jéquier, ibid., pp. 19–26 and pl. VI; also *Douze ans de fouilles*, pp. 144–6.

174 Jéquier, *Douze ans de fouilles*, p. 145.

175 Ibid., p. 146, also *Deux pyramides du Moyen Empire*, pl. V, (*b, c*).

176 Jéquier, *Douze ans de fouilles*, p. 155.

CHAPTER IX

177 Lauer and Sainte Fare Garnot, 'Rapport préliminaire sur les recherches entreprises dans le sous-sol de la pyramide de Téti à Saqqarah en 1951 et 1955/1956', *ASAE*, LV, pp. 253–61 and 2 plates.

178 *BSFE*, 43, pp. 18–19 and pl. B facing p. 13.

179 Lauer, in *CRAIB*, 1966, pp. 461–9 and fig. 2; also in *BSFE*, 47, pp. 26–32 and pl. III.

180 *CRAIB*, 1966, pp. 467–8 and pl. III (B); also Leclant in *BSFE*, 46, pl. III, and in *OR*, 36, 2, pls. XXVI–XXVIII.

181 *CRAIB*, 1969, pp. 466–7 and pl. II; *BSFE*, 52, pp. 23–7 and pl. IV; also Leclant in *OR*, 37, 1, pls. XXIV–XXVI; 38, 2, pls. XXII–XXV, and 39, 2, pls. XXXIV–XXXVII.

182 Lauer and Leclant, 'Découverte de statues de prisonniers au temple de la pyramide de Pépi Ier', in *RE*, 21, pp. 55–62; also Lauer, in *CRAIB*, 1969, pp. 468–79 and pls. III–VI, and in *BSFE*, 56, pp. 17–24, and pls. II, III; also Leclant, in *OR*, 39, 2, pls. XXVII–XXXII.

183 Lauer, in *CRAIB*, 1970, p. 491 and pl. V (*a, b*); also Leclant in *OR*, 40, 2, pp. 232–3 and pl. XXVI, fig. 15.

184 Leclant in *BSFE*, 58, pp. 5–18 and figures.

185 Lauer, in *BSFE*, 62.

186 Lauer, in *CRAIB*, 1970, p. 498, and plan, fig. 3.

187 Ibid., pp. 498–502, and pl. IX (*c*).

188 *BSFE*, 62.

CHAPTER X

189 W. B. Emery's annual reports in *JEA*, 51 (1965) to 56 (1970).

190 Emery, *JEA*, 52, p. 8, in which he notes that Nefertum, as the son of Ptah, was identified with Imhotep during the Ptolemaic period.

191 Emery, in *JEA*, 55, pls. VI, VII and VIII (5, 6).

192 Ibid., pl. VIII (1–4). Emery points out (pp. 33–4) that Belzoni discovered such false animal mummies during his explorations at Thebes; see G. Belzoni, *Narrative of Operations* (London 1820), I, p. 261 f. and pl. 44.

193 Ibid., pl. IX (2).

194 Emery, in *JEA*, 56, pl. X (1).

195 Ibid., p. 7.

196 Ibid., pl. XIV (2, 3).

197 Ibid., pl. XV.

198 Ibid., pl. XVI (1). Emery had compared (p. 8) these plaster casts with similar terracotta objects from the temple of Aesculapius in Rome, now in the Wellcome Institute of the History of Medicine, London; three of these masks are reproduced in his pl. XVI (2).

199 Ibid., pl. XVII (1).

# Bibliography

## LIST OF ABBREVIATIONS

| | |
|---|---|
| *AÖAW* | *Anzeiger der philosophisch-historischen Klasse, Öster-reichische Akademie der Wissenschaften,* Vienna |
| *ASAE* | *Annales du Service des Antiquités de l'Egypte,* Cairo |
| *Beiträge Bf.* | *Beiträge zur ägyptischen Bauforschung und Altertums-kunde,* Cairo |
| *BIE* | *Bulletin de l'Institut d'Egypte,* Cairo |
| *BIFAO* | *Bulletin de l'Institut français d'archéologie orientale du Caire,* Cairo |
| *BSFE* | *Bulletin de la Société française d'égyptologie,* Paris |
| *CdE* | *Chronique d'Egypte,* Brussels |
| *CRAIB* | *Comptes rendus de l'Académie des Inscriptions et Belles-Lettres,* Paris |
| *IFAO* | Institut français d'archéologie orientale du Caire, Cairo |
| *JAOS* | *Journal of the American Oriental Society,* Chicago |
| *JEA* | *The Journal of Egyptian Archaeology,* London |
| *JNES* | *Journal of Near Eastern Studies,* Chicago |
| *MDAIK* | *Mitteilungen des Deutschen Instituts für ägyptische Alter-tumskunde in Kairo,* Wiesbaden |
| *OLZ* | *Orientalistische Literaturzeitung,* Berlin |
| *OR* | *Orientalia,* Rome |
| *RA* | *Revue archéologique,* Paris |
| *RE* | *Revue d'égyptologie,* Paris |
| *Rec. de Trav.* | *Recueil de travaux relatifs à la philologie et à l'archéologie égyptienne et assyrienne,* 3–14, Paris 1882–93 |
| *Suppl. ASAE* | *Supplément aux Annales du Service des Antiquités de l'Egypte* (numbered volumes), Cairo |
| *ZÄS* | *Zeitschrift für ägyptische Sprache und Altertumskunde,* Leipzig |

# GENERAL WORKS

| | |
|---|---|
| ALDRED, C. | *The Development of Egyptian Art*, 3 vols., London 1949–51. |
| BADAWY, AL | *Le dessin architectural chez les anciens Egyptiens*, Cairo 1948. |
| ——— | *A History of Egyptian Architecture*, I, Giza 1954; II, III, University of California Press 1966, 1968. |
| BREASTED, J. H. | *Ancient Records of Egypt*, I–IV, Chicago 1906–7. |
| ——— | *The Development of Religion and Thought in Ancient Egypt*, New York 1912. |
| CAPART, J. | *Memphis, à l'ombre des Pyramides*, Brussels 1930. |
| ——— | *L'Art Egyptien*, 2 vols., Brussels 1909–11. Also *Deuxième Partie*, I, *L'Architecture*, 1922; II, *La Statuaire*, 1948; III, *Les Arts graphiques*, 1942; IV, *Les Arts mineurs*, 1947. |
| DRIOTON, ET. and VANDIER, J. | *Les Peuples de l'Orient méditerranéen*, II, *L'Egypte*, 3rd ed., Paris 1952. |
| EDWARDS, I. E. S. | 'The early dynastic period in Egypt', in *The Cambridge Ancient History*, vol. I, ch. XI. |
| ——— | *The Pyramids of Egypt*, Harmondsworth, revised ed., 1972. |
| EMERY, W. B. | *Archaic Egypt*, Harmondsworth 1961. |
| FAKHRY, A. | *The Pyramids*, Chicago 1961. |
| FRANKFORT, H. | *Kingship and the Gods*, Chicago 1948. |
| GARDINER, A. H. | *The attitude of the ancient Egyptians to death and the dead*, Cambridge 1935. |
| GIEDION, S. | *The Eternal Present: The Beginning of Architecture*, London and New York 1964. |
| GRINSELL, L. V. | *Egyptian Pyramids*, Gloucester 1947. |
| HAYES, W. C. | *The Scepter of Egypt*, 2 vols., New York and Cambridge, 1953–9. |
| HELK, W. | 'Pyramiden', in Pauly-Kroll-Ziegler, *Real-Encyclo-pädie der klassischen Altertums-Wissenschaft*, XXIII, 2, col. 2167–282. |
| JÉQUIER, G. | *Manuel d'archéologie égyptienne*, Paris 1924. |
| JUNKER, H. | *Pyramidenzeit. Das Wesen der Altägyptischen Religion*, Zurich 1949. |
| KEES, H. | *Der Götterglaube in alten Aegypten*, Leipzig 1941. |
| ——— | *Totenglauben und Jenseits-Vorstellungen der alten Ägypter*, 2nd ed., Berlin 1956. |
| LANGE, K. and HIRMER, M. | *Egypt: Architecture, Sculpture, Painting in three thousand years*, 4th ed., London 1968. |
| LAUER, J.-Ph. | *Le problème des pyramides d'Egypte*, Paris 1948 and 1952. |
| ——— | *Histoire monumentale des pyramides d'Egypte*, I, *Les pyramides à degrés (IIIe. dynastie)*, in *Bibliothèque d'Etude de l'IFAO*, XXXIX (1962). |
| ——— | *Le mystère des pyramides*, Paris 1974. |
| LUCAS, A. | *Ancient Egyptian Materials and Industries*, 3rd ed., London 1948. |

| | |
|---|---|
| MONTET, P. | *Eternal Egypt*, New York 1964. |
| PORTER, B. and MOSS, R. | *Topographical Bibliography of Ancient Egyptian Hieroglyphic Texts, Reliefs and Paintings*, III, *Memphis*, Oxford 1931. |
| PETRIE, W. M. F. | *A History of Egypt*, I, *From the earliest kings to the XVIth Dynasty*, 10th ed., London 1923. |
| POSENER, G. | *A Dictionary of Egyptian Civilization*, London 1962. |
| PRISSE D'AVENNES | *Histoire de l'art égyptien d'après les monuments*, Paris 1878. |
| RANKE, H. | *The Art of Ancient Egypt*, Vienna 1936. |
| REISNER, G. A. | *The Development of the Egyptian Tomb down to the Accession of Cheops*, Cambridge, Mass. 1936. |
| SCHÄFER, H. and ANDREAE, W. | *Die Kunst des alten Orients*, 3rd ed., Berlin 1932. |
| SMITH, E. B. | *Egyptian Architecture as a Cultural Expression*, New York 1938. |
| SMITH, W. S. | *A History of Egyptian Sculpture and Painting in the Old Kingdom*, Oxford 1946. |
| ——— | *The Art and Architecture of Ancient Egypt*, London and Baltimore 1958. |
| ——— | 'The Old Kingdom in Egypt', in *The Cambridge Ancient History*, vol. I, ch. XIV. |
| STEINDORFF, G. | *Die Kunst der Ägypter*, Leipzig 1928. |
| VANDIER, J. | *Manuel d'archéologie égyptienne*, 5 vols., Paris 1952–70. |
| WILSON, J. | *The Burden of Egypt*, Chicago 1951. |

## OTHER WORKS AND ARTICLES CONCERNING SAQQARA

| | |
|---|---|
| ALDRED, C. | *Egypt to the End of the Old Kingdom*, London and New York 1965. |
| ——— | *Jewels of the Pharaohs: Egyptian Jewellery of the Dynastic Period*, London and New York 1972. |
| BADAWI, AHMED M. | 'Denkmäler aus Sakkarah', *ASAE*, XL–XLII. |
| ——— | 'Das Gräberfeld in der Nähe der Mastaba des Ptahhetep', *ASAE*, XL. |
| BADAWY, AL | 'Architectural Devices against the Violation of Egyptian Tombs', *Bull. Fac. of Arts, Cairo University*, XVI, 1 (1954). |
| ——— | 'La stèle funéraire sous L'Ancien Empire, son origine et son fonctionnement', *ASAE*, XLVIII. |
| BARSANTI, A. and MASPERO, G. | 'Fouilles autour de la pyramide d'Ounas', *ASAE*, I, III and V. |
| BELLEW, P. and SCHUTZ, A. | *Egypte, peinture des tombeaux et des temples*, with an Introduction by J. Vandier, Paris 1954. |
| BISSING, F. W. VON and WEIGALL, A. E. P. | *Die Mastaba des Gem-ni-kai*, 2 vols., Berlin 1905, Leipzig 1911. |
| BORCHARDT, L. | 'Zur Geschichte der Pyramiden. VIII. Weiteres zur Baugeschichte der Stufenmastaba bei Saqqara', *ZÄS*, 73, 2. |

| | |
|---|---|
| | 'Aufnahmen der Inschriften in der Mastaba el-Faraun', *OLZ*, XXXIV. |
| | *Die Entstehung der Pyramide an der Baugeschichte der Pyramide bei Mejdum nachgewiesen*, Berlin 1928. |
| BOREUX, CH. | 'Etudes de nautique égyptienne. L'art de la navigation en Egypte jusqu'à la fin de l'Ancien Empire', *Mémoires IFAO*, 50, Cairo 1925. |
| BRUNTON, G. | 'The burial of Prince Ptah-Shepses at Saqqara', *ASAE*, XLVII. |
| CAPART, J. | *Une rue de Tombeaux à Saqqarah*, 2 vols., Brussels 1907. |
| | 'À Saqqarah', *CdE*, 4 (1927). |
| | 'Fouilles de Saqqarah. La pyramide de Djéser et l'œuvre d'Imhotep', *CdE*, 8 (1929). |
| | *Documents pour servir à l'étude de l'art égyptien*, 2 vols., Paris 1927–31. |
| | *Memphis à l'ombre des pyramides*, Brussels 1930. |
| | *Propos sur l'art égyptien*, Brussels 1931. |
| CLARKE, S. and ENGELBACH, R. | *Ancient Egyptian Masonry*, London 1930. |
| DAVIES, N. DE G. | *The mastaba of Ptahhetep and Akhethetep*, 2 vols., London 1900–1. |
| DAVIES, N. M. and GARDINER, A. H. | *Ancient Egyptian Paintings*, 3 vols., Chicago 1936. |
| DERRY, D. E. | 'The bones of Prince Ptah-Shepses', *ASAE*, XLVII. |
| DRIOTON, E. | Articles concerning Saqqara in *ASAE*, XLIII–XLV, LI, LII; *BIE*, XXV, XXVI; *CRAIB*, 1947; *ASAE*, XXXVI, LI, LV. |
| DRIOTON, E. and LAUER, J.-PH. | *The Pyramids of Sakkarah*, Cairo 1939, 1951. |
| DRIOTON, E. and VIGNEAU, A. | *Le Musée du Caire*, Paris 1949. |
| DUELL, P. | *The Mastaba of Mereruka*. Parts 1 and 2 (Oriental Institute Publications, vols. 31, 39), Chicago 1938. |
| EMERY, W. B. | *The Tomb of Hemaka*, with the collaboration of Zaki Y. Saad, Cairo 1938. |
| | *Excavations at Saqqara, 1937–1938. Hor-Aha*, with the collaboration of Zaki Y. Saad, Cairo 1939. |
| | *Great Tombs of the First Dynasty*, I, Cairo 1949; II, London, 1954; III, London, 1958. |
| | Articles concerning Saqqara in *ASAE*, XXXVIII, XXXIX, XLV; *JEA*, vols. 51–6. |
| EPERON, L., DAUMAS, F. and GOYON, G. | *Le tombeau de Ti: Dessins et aquarelles*, I, Cairo 1939. |
| ERMAN, A. | *Reden, Rufe und Lieder auf Gräberbildern des Alten Reiches*, Berlin 1919. |
| FAULKNER, R. O. | *The Ancient Egyptian Pyramid Texts*, 2 vols., Oxford 1969. |
| FIRTH, C. M. | Articles on Saqqara in *ASAE*, XXIV–XXXI. |
| FIRTH, C. M. and GUNN, B. | *The Teti Pyramid Cemeteries*, 2 vols., Cairo 1926. |

FIRTH, C. M. and    *The Step Pyramid*, 2 vols., Cairo 1935.
QUIBELL, J. E.

FISCHER, H. G.    'A Scribe of the army in a Saqqara mastaba of the
early Fifth Dynasty', *JNES*, XVIII/4, 1959.
———    'The Butcher Ph-r-ntr', *OR*, 29, fasc. 2, 1960.
———    'An Egyptian royal stela of the second dynasty',
*Artibus Asiae*, XXIV/1, Ascona 1961.

GONEIM, M.    *The Buried Pyramid*, London 1964.
ZAKARIA

———    *Horus Sekhem-khet: The Unfinished Step Pyramid at
Saqqara*, I, Cairo 1957.

GOYON, G.    'Les navires de transport de la chaussée monumentale
d'Ounas', *BIFAO*, LXIX, 1971.

GUNN, B.    'The inscribed sarcophagi in the Serapeum', *ASAE*,
XXVI.

———    'Inscriptions from the Step Pyramid site', *ASAE*,
XXVI, XXVIII, XXXV.

HASSAN, S.    'Excavations at Saqqara (1937–1938)', *ASAE*,
XXXVIII.

———    'The Causeway of Wnis at Saqqara', *ZÄS*, 80.

HERMANN, A.    *Führer durch die Altertümer von Memphis und Sakkara*,
Berlin 1938.

HURRY, J. B.    *Imhotep*, Oxford 1926.

HUSSEIN, ABDEL    'Fouilles sur la chaussée d'Ounas (1941–1942)',
SALAM M.    *ASAE*, XLIII.

———    'The reparation of the mastaba of Mehu at Saqqara',
*ASAE*, XLII.

JÉQUIER, G.    *Le Mastabat Faraoun*, with the collaboration of Dows
Dunham, Cairo 1928.
———    *La pyramide d'Oudjebten*, Cairo 1928.
———    *Tombeaux de particuliers contemporains de Pépi II*, Cairo
1928.
———    *Les pyramides des reines Neit et Apouit*, Cairo 1933.
———    *La pyramide d'Aba*, Cairo 1935.
———    *Deux pyramides du Moyen Empire*, Cairo 1938.
———    *Le monument funéraire de Pépi II*, 3 vols., Cairo 1936–40.
———    Articles on Saqqara in *ASAE*, XXV–XXXVI.
———    'Les stèles de Djeser', *CdE*, 27.
———    *Douze ans de fouilles dans la nécropole memphite, 1924–
1936*, Neuchâtel 1940.

JUNKER, H.    'Von der ägyptischen Baukunst des Alten Reiches',
*ZÄS*, 63.
———    'Zu dem Idealbild des menschlichen Körpers in der
Kunst des Alten Reiches', *AOAW*, 84 (1947).
———    'Das lebenswahre Bildnis in der Rundplastik des
Alten Reiches', *AOAW*, 87 (1950).

KAISER, W.    'Zu den königlichen Tabelzirken der 1. und 2.
Dynastie in Abydos und zur Baugeschichte des
Djoser-Grabmals', *MDAIK*, 25 (1969).

LACAU, P.    'Suppressions et modifications de signes dans les
textes funéraires', *ZÄS*, 51 (1914).

235

—————— 'Suppressions des noms divins dans les textes de la chambre funéraire', *ASAE*, XXVI (1926).

—————— 'Le panier de pêche égyptien', *BIFAO*, LIV (1954).

LACAU, P. and LAUER, J.-PH.   In *Fouilles à Saqqarah* (IFAO): *La Pyramide à degrés, IV, Inscriptions gravées sur les vases*, 2 fasc., Cairo 1959, 1961; V, *Inscriptions à l'encre sur les vases*, Cairo 1965.

LAUER, J.-PH.   In *Fouilles à Saqqarah* (Service des Antiquités de l'Egypte): *La Pyramide à degrés. L'architecture*, I (text), II (plates), Cairo 1936; III, *Compléments*, Cairo 1939.

—————— 'Reconstitution de l'ordre fasciculé de Saqqarah (IIIème. dynastie)', *Mémoires de l'IFAO*, XXXV (Mélanges Maspero).

—————— 'Étude sur quelques monuments de la IIIème. dynastie', *ASAE*, XXVII–XXXII.

—————— 'Études complémentaires sur les monuments du roi Zoser à Saqqarah', *Supplément ASAE*, No. 9, Cairo 1948.

—————— 'Fouilles du Service des Antiquités à Saqqarah', *ASAE*, XXXIII–XXXIX, LIII.

—————— 'Rapports sur les restaurations effectuées dans les monuments de Zoser à Saqqarah', *ASAE*, XXX–XXXIX, LIV, LVII.

—————— 'Le temple haut de la pyramide du roi Ouserkaf à Saqqarah', *ASAE*, LIII.

—————— 'Restaurations et "anastylose" dans les monuments du roi Zoser à Saqqarah (1927–1947)', *ASAE*, XLVIII.

—————— 'Remarques sur les stèles fausses-portes de l'Horus Neteri-khet sous la Pyramide à degrés et son enceinte Sud', in *Monuments Piot*, 49.

—————— 'Observations sur les pyramides', in *Biblioth. d'Etude de l'IFAO*, XXX (1960).

—————— 'Mariette à Saqqarah, du Sérapéum à la Direction des Antiquités, in *Biblioth. d'Etude de l'IFAO*, XXXII (Mélanges Mariette).

—————— *The pyramids of Sakkarah*, Cairo 1961, 1971.

—————— Articles concerning Saqqara in *BIE*, XXXIV, XXXVI, XXXVIII, XLVII–XLIX; *BIFAO*, XLI, LIX, LXI, LXIV; *BSFE*, 9, 12, 18, 22, 33, 37–8, 40, 43, 47, 52, 56, 62; *OR*, 35, 38; *RA*, 1957, 1959; *RE*, 7, 14, 15.

—————— 'La résurrection des monuments du roi Zoser à Saqqarah', *CRAIB*, 1950.

—————— 'L'apport historique des récentes découvertes du Service des Antiquités de l'Egypte dans la nécropole memphite', *CRAIB*, 1954.

—————— 'L'œuvre d'Imhotep à Saqqarah', *CRAIB*, 1956.

—————— 'Recherches et travaux dans la nécropole de Saqqarah', *CRAIB*, 1963, 1966, 1967, 1969, 1970, 1972, 1973.

———— 'Evolution de la tombe royale égyptienne jusqu'à la Pyramide à degrés', *MDAIK*, 15.

———— 'Sondages dans la région Sud du complexe funéraire de l'Horus Sekhem-khet à Saqqarah', *ASAE*, LIX.

———— 'Recherche et découverte du tombeau Sud de l'Horus Sekhem-khet dans son complexe funéraire à Saqqarah', *RE*, 20.

LAUER, J.-PH. and DEBONO, F. 'Technique du façonnage des croissants de silex utilisés dans l'enceinte de Zoser à Saqqarah', *ASAE*, 2.

LAUER, J.-PH. and DERRY, D. E. 'Découverte à Saqqarah d'une partie de la momie du roi Zoser', *ASAE*, XXXV.

LAUER, J.-PH. and ISKANDAR, Z. 'Données nouvelles sur la momification dans l'Egypte ancienne', *ASAE*, LIII.

LAUER, J.-PH. and LECLANT, J. *Le temple haut du complexe funéraire du roi Téti*, Cairo 1972.

———— 'Découverte de statues de prisonniers au temple de Pépi Ier.', *RE*, 21 (1969).

LAUER, J.-PH. and PICARD, CH. 'Les statues ptolémaïques du Sarapieion de Memphis', *Publications de l'Institut d'Art et d'Archéologie de de l'Université de Paris*, III (1955).

LAUER, J.-PH. and SAINTE FARE GARNOT, J. 'Rapport préliminaire sur les recherches entreprises dans le sous-sol de la pyramide de Téti à Saqqarah en 1951 et 1955/56', *ASAE*, LV.

LAUER, J.-PH., LAURENT-TÄCKHOLM, V. and ÄBERG, E. 'Les plantes découvertes dans les souterrains de l'enceinte du roi Zoser à Saqqarah', *BIE*, XXXII (1950).

LECLANT, J. Reports on works at Saqqara in *BSFE*, 46, 58.

———— 'Fouilles et travaux en Egypte', *OR*, 19, 21, 22, 24, 27, 30, 32–40.

———— 'Le rôle du lait et de l'allaitement d'après les Textes des pyramides', *JNES*, X, 2 (1951).

LHOTE, A. *Les chefs d'œuvre de la peinture égyptienne*, Paris 1954.

LORET, V. 'Fouilles dans la nécropole memphite (1897–1899)', *Bull. Inst. Egyptien*, III, No. 10, Cairo 1899.

MACRAMALLAH, R. In *Fouilles à Saqqarah* (Service des Antiquités de l'Egypte): *Le Mastaba de Idout*, Cairo 1935; *Un cimetière archaïque de la classe moyenne du peuple à Saqqarah*, Cairo 1940.

MALININE, M., POSENER, G., and VERCOUTTER, J. *Catalogue des stèles du Sérapéum de Memphis*, 2 vols. (text and plates), Paris 1968.

MARAGIOGLIO, V. and RINALDI, C. *Notizie sulle piramidi di Zedefra, Zedkara Isesi, Teti*, Turin 1962.

———— *L'architettura delle Piramidi Menfite*, II, Turin 1963, and VI, Rapallo 1967.

MARIETTE, A. *Le Sérapéum de Memphis, 1857*, text, Paris 1882.

———— *Les mastabas de l'Ancien Empire* (completed by G. Maspero), Paris 1885.

| | |
|---|---|
| MARTIN, G. T. | 'Excavations in the Sacred Animal Necropolis at North Saqqara, 1971–2: Preliminary Report', *JEA*, 59 (1973), and 'Excavations . . . at North Saqqara, 1972–3: Preliminary Report', *JEA*, 60 (1974). |
| MASPERO, G. | 'La pyramide du roi Ounas', *Rec. de Trav.*, III, IV. |
| ———— | 'La pyramide du roi Téti', *Rec. de Trav.*, V. |
| ———— | 'La pyramide du roi Pépi Ier', *Rec. de Trav.*, V. |
| ———— | 'La pyramide du roi Mirinri Ier', *Rec. de Trav.*, IX, X, XI. |
| ———— | 'La pyramide du roi Pépi II', *Rec. de Trav.*, XII, XIV. |
| ———— | 'Trois années de fouilles', *Mém. Miss. fr. Caire*, I, Cairo 1884. |
| ———— | *Les inscriptions des pyramides de Saqqarah*, Paris 1894. |
| MEKHITARIAN, A. | *Egyptian Painting*, Geneva 1954. |
| MINUTOLI, General VON | *Reise zum Tempel des Jupiter Ammon*, 1821. |
| MONTET, P. | *Scènes de la vie privée dans les tombeaux égyptiens de l'Ancien Empire*, Paris and Strasbourg 1925. |
| ———— | 'La fabrication du vin dans les tombeaux antérieurs au Nouvel Empire', *Rec. de Trav.*, XXXV. |
| MORGAN, J. DE | *Carte de la Nécropole Memphite*, Cairo 1897. |
| MURRAY, M. A. | *Saqqara Mastabas*, London 1905. |
| ———— | *Index of Names and Titles of the Old Kingdom*, London 1908. |
| NIMS, F. | 'Some notes on the family of Mereruka', *JAOS*, 58/4. |
| PERRING, J. S. | *The Pyramids of Gizeh*, part III, London 1842. |
| PICARD, C. | 'Le Pindare de l'Exèdre des poètes et des sages au Serapeion de Memphis', *Monuments Piot*, 46. |
| QUIBELL, J. E. | *Excavations at Saqqara (1905–1906)*, Cairo 1907. |
| ———— | *Excavations at Saqqara (1906–1907)* (with a section of religious texts by P. Lacau), Cairo 1908. |
| ———— | *Excavations at Saqqara (1907–1908)*, Cairo 1909. |
| ———— | *Excavations at Saqqara (1908–9, 1909–10). The Monastery of Apia Jeremias*, Cairo 1912. |
| ———— | *Excavations at Saqqara (1911–1912). The tomb of Hesy*, Cairo 1913. |
| ———— | *Excavations at Saqqara (1912–1914). Archaic Mastabas*, Cairo 1923. |
| ———— | 'Stone vessels from the Step Pyramid', *ASAE*, XXXV. |
| QUIBELL, J. E. and HAYTER, A. G. K. | *Excavations at Saqqara. Teti Pyramid, North Side*, Cairo 1927. |
| RICKE, H. | 'Bemerkungen zur ägyptischen Baukunst des Alten Reiches', I, *Beiträge Bf.*, 4, Zurich 1944; II, *Beiträge Bf.*, 5, Cairo 1950. |
| RHONÉ, A. | *L'Egypte à petites journées*, Paris, new ed. 1910. |
| SAINTE FARE GARNOT, J. | 'L'appel aux vivants dans les textes funéraires égyptiens des origines à la fin de l'Ancien Empire', *Rech. d'archéol. de Philol. et d'Hist.*, IX, Cairo 1938. |

|  |  |
|---|---|
| —— | 'Quelques aspects du parallélisme dans les Textes des pyramides', *Rev. d'hist. des religions*, 123 (1941). |
| —— | *Les fonctions, les pouvoirs et la nature du nom propre dans l'Ancienne Egypte d'après les Textes des pyramides*, Paris 1948. |
| —— | *L'hommage aux dieux sous l'Ancien Empire, d'après les Textes des pyramides*, Paris 1954. |
| —— | 'Sur quelques noms royaux des IIe. et IIIe. dynasties égyptiennes', *BIE*, XXXVII (1956). |
| SCHÄFER, H. | 'Das Reliefschmuck der Berliner Tür aus der Stufenpyramide und der Königstitel *Hr-nb*', *MDAIK*, 4/1 (1933). |
| SCHARFF, A. | *Das Grab als Wohnhaus in der ägyptischen Frühzeit*, Munich 1947. |
| SCHOTT, S. | 'Bemerkungen zum ägyptischen Pyramidenkult', *Beiträge Bf.*, 5, Cairo 1950. |
| —— | 'Aufnahmen vom Hungersnotrelief aus dem Aufweg der Unaspyramide', *RE*, 17 (1965). |
| SEGATO, G. and VALERIANI, D. | *Atlante monumentale del Basso e dell'Alto Egitto*, 2 vols., Florence 1837, 1838. |
| SERVIN, A. | 'Constructions navales égyptiennes. Les barques de papyrus', *ASAE*, XLVIII. |
| SETHE, K. | *Die altägyptischen Pyramidentexte*, 3 vols., Leipzig 1908–22. |
| —— | *Übersetzung und Kommentar zu den altägyptischen Pyramiden Texten*, 6 vols., Gluckstadt 1935–62. |
| —— | 'Imhotep, der Asklepios der Aegypter', *Untersuchungen zur Geschichte und Altertumskunde Aegyptens*, II. |
| SHOUKRY, M. ANWAR | 'Die Privatgrabstatue im Alten Reich', in *Suppl. ASAE*, 15 (1951). |
| SIMPSON, W. K. | 'A statuette of King Nyneter', *JEA*, 42 (1956). |
| SMITH, H. S. | *A Visit in Ancient Egypt*, Warminster 1974. |
| SPEELERS, L. | *Traduction, index et vocabulaire des Textes des pyramides égyptiennes*, Brussels 1935. |
| STEINDORF, G. | *Das Grab des Ti*, Leipzig 1913. |
| VANDIER, J. | See under General Works above. |
| VERCOUTTER, J. | 'Une épitaphe royale inédite du Sérapéum', *MDAIK*, 16 (1958). |
| —— | *Textes biographiques du Sérapéum de Memphis*, Paris 1962. |
| VYSE, H. | Appendix to *Operations carried on at the Pyramids of Gizeh in 1837*, Vol. III, 1842. |
| WALL, B. VAN DE | 'Remarques sur l'origine et le sens des défilés de domaines dans les mastabas de l'Ancien Empire', *MDAIK*, 15/1. |
| —— | 'L'érection du pilier djed', *La Nouvelle Clio*, 5–6, Brussels 1954. |
| WALLON, M. H. | *Notice sur la vie et les travaux de François-Auguste-Ferdinand Mariette-Pacha*, (Institut de France), Paris 1883. |

SAQQARA

| | |
|---|---|
| WEILL, R. | 'Les origines de l'Egypte pharaonique. La IIème et IIIème dynasties égyptiennes', *Annales du Musée Guimet*, XXV, Paris 1908. |
| —— | 'Le roi Neterkhet-Zeser et l'officier Imhotep à la pyramide à degrés de Saqqarah', *Revue de l'Egypte ancienne*, II (1928). |
| WILD, H. | *Le tombeau de Ti*, fasc. II, *La chapelle (première partie)*, Cairo 1953. |
| —— | *Le tombeau de Ti*, fasc. III, *La chapelle (deuxième partie)*, Cairo 1966. |
| —— | 'La danse dans l'Egypte ancienne. Les documents figurés', *Position des thèses des Elèves de l'Ecole du Louvre (1911–1944)*, Paris 1956. |
| WRESZINSKI, W. | *Atlas zur Altägyptischen Kulturgeschichte*, III, 3 vols., Leipzig 1936–8. |
| YOYOTTE, J. | 'A propos de la parenté féminine du roi Téti (VIe. dyn.)', *BIFAO*, LVII (1958). |
| ŽÁBA, ZBYNÉK | *Les Maximes de Ptahhotep*, Prague 1956. |

# Sources of Illustrations

All photographs are by Albert Shoucair except as listed below.

J.-Ph. Lauer   60, 78, 79, 82, 83, 85, 88, 90, 91, 93–5, 102–9, 117–19, 152–65
Archives Photographiques, Paris   29
Peter Clayton   168, 169
Courtesy, Egypt Exploration Society   75, 76, 166, 167, 170, 174; courtesy, Egypt Exploration Society and Department of Egyptology, University College, London (objects in the Flinders Petrie Collection)   171 (UC 30491), 172 (UC 30489), 173 (UC 30479), 175 (UC 30476) – photos 171–3 Peter Clayton
Professor Max Hirmer   15
Louvre, Paris   6, 7, 10, 13, 14
Service des Antiquités d'Egypte   1, 2, 4, 5, 8, 25, 28, 77, 80, 81, 84, 86, 87, 89, 92, 97–101, 103, 104, 106, 112–16, 120–4, 126, 127, 134–41, 147–50
R. Toulon   26, 27
Roger Wood   12

# Index